LAUNCH Your New CAREER

Advance Praise

"What I appreciate *most* about Carine's book is that she shares an excellent step-by-step manual to become wildly successful!

I have learned many skills already since December 2018 after attending DWD in Florida. On the last day of the event my hubby and I had the pleasure of meeting Carine.

Little did I know that she was going to write a simple yet powerful how-to book that shows the ways and why's of building your own financial freedom business.

Everything she writes is easy to understand and implement.

Carine has provided me with a road map for finally leaving a dreadful corporate job and systematically start working to build my own business.

Is it because of the fact that this book was written by a woman or is it because Carine is "just a small-town girl" who used to live in that same "small country and small town" where I live today that makes this book resonate with me?

Thank you very much, Carine. Your life experience gives me the confidence to move forward and I feel I can knock years off my learning curve as I strive to build a lucrative and successful business.

As Carine quotes in her book: 'When is NOW a good time to start?'

Oh, right! NOW!!! So, let's get going!"

– **Christelle Pieteraerens**, Distributor at Foreverliving

"I could not put this book down! Carine reinforced for me that eighty percent of your success is mindset and only twenty percent is strategy. Her relevant stories, tools, and humor masterfully outlined exactly what the new coach needs to step into their power and "do" their emotions to get the results they desire—a lucrative, successful coaching practice. It resonated and inspired me when she describes in detail the recipe for success that her clients demonstrate, which includes not only a positive mindset, but rituals, accountability, massive action, and the clarity of *why* the coach is passionate about helping their clients.

This book is a must for new coaches just starting as well as existing coaches who want to take their businesses to the next level!!"

– **Sandi Boyd**, coach and CEO of Revivify Coaching and Consulting

"As the title says, this is the best book for those starting out as a life coach looking to sign up clients, but also a great read for established life coaches trying to take their coaching practice to the next level. Not only does Carine provide thought-provoking and mind-strengthening tools for your own coaching practice, she also highlights tools to enhance and better your personal life.

Sign Up Your First Coaching Client is not a book that you can just read. Carine repeatedly instructs us to "Now go write! You will thank me later" throughout the book, making sure you are actually interacting, instead of passively reading.

These amazing tools has provided me with much clarity on where I am in my journey to becoming the most effective life coach and the best version of me that I can be!!"

– **Hussein Yassine**, Coach

LAUNCH
Your New
CAREER

STEPS TO SIGNING UP
YOUR FIRST CLIENT

Carine Kindinger

NEW YORK

LONDON • NASHVILLE • MELBOURNE • VANCOUVER

LAUNCH Your New CAREER
STEPS TO SIGNING UP YOUR FIRST CLIENT

Published in New York, New York, by Morgan James Publishing in partnership with Difference Press. Morgan James is a trademark of Morgan James, LLC. www.MorganJamesPublishing.com

ISBN 978-1-64279-966-8 paperback
ISBN 978-1-64279-967-5 eBook
ISBN 978-1-64279-968-2 audio
Library of Congress Control Number: 2019920212

Cover Design Concept:
Jennifer Stimson

Cover Design by:
Rachel Lopez
www.r2cdesign.com

Editor:
Bethany Davis

Book Coaching:
The Author Incubator

Morgan James is a proud partner of Habitat for Humanity Peninsula and Greater Williamsburg. Partners in building since 2006.

Get involved today! Visit
www.MorganJamesBuilds.com

This book is for Veronique.
Sis, thank you inspiring me to be better every day
and to step up no matter what is going on in my life.

TABLE OF CONTENTS

CHAPTER 1
I HEAR YOU!

"If you hear a voice within you say 'you cannot paint,'
then by all means paint, and that voice will be silenced."
– Vincent Van Gogh

Aim, aim…will you fire?

Do you know the expression "aim, aim, aim…but never fire?" Well, that was me. Until now. And it is probably you, too. You know deep in your heart that your next step is to start your new coaching career. To leave your current job and to launch.

Yet, like many, you are afraid to start. And then come all the questions that are cluttering your mind endlessly. What if you don't have what it takes? What if you spend all your resources, money, time, energy, and so on for nothing? What if you fail? What if you don't have what it takes to be successful at this next business? What would your husband say? What impact will this have on your family? Could you even look at yourself in the mirror if it does not work out? The fear is real.

Maybe your mama was right when she advised you to just stick to your current job, that you do not need to put yourself out there. That all you need is job security, and nothing else is essential. She (or someone else in your close friends and family) might have even played the health insurance card—and probably the retirement card. "Certainty is key, dear. How many more times do I need to tell you?" I'll bet you heard that one!

And now here you are, feeling lost and somewhat stuck. You know there is more out there. You know that you were born to make a difference. You feel it in your heart. You know it is your life's purpose. Perhaps you have not even gone so far as to name it your life's purpose. Yet you feel the gap within you, and you know that living the life you have right now, working at this job every day, is not going to work any longer.

You are done. You want more. You want to follow your heart. The Universe, or perhaps you call it a Higher Power, put a dream in your heart, a burning desire. You know you must go after it, but…you feel stuck. Where to even start? Is it even possible? You are asking yourself, "How am I going to open this new business while still paying the bills?" And you freeze. You might have even put your dream on hold for years, like I did with my own coaching business.

I have great news for you: you are in the right place. I've got your back! I am going to take you on your own journey to equip you with the tools needed to open your own business. My promise to you is that this works! One of my dear clients said to me in our last coaching session, "Coach, if only I had put into practice all that you shared with me over this past year, I would be so much further. You were right all along!"

The Dream

I have always dreamed of writing a book one day. And it was going to start with four magic words: "Once upon a time ..."

I had this dream in my heart for years—over twenty years to be exact. And every year, I thought of a title, or some content I wanted to share. Then I would imagine the cover of this fantastic book, and I would see myself doing speaking events and sharing the book with the people around me. I knew I had to write a book that would make a difference. That would really impact people.

For the last twenty years or so, I have known that my mission in life is to empower people to become who they were born to be. And I waited and waited, finding excuses one after another! Sound like anyone you know?

What else are you not going after and putting on hold in your life? I know you want to live your own dream more than anything else right now. I know you are craving fulfillment and growth. You feel that something is missing, and you cannot ignore it any longer.

You picked up this book for a reason. Don't say "no" to yourself any longer. Let's do this together.

The tools and strategies shared in the following pages will take you to new heights. My question to you is, "Are you ready?" And if your answer is yes, then let's do this.

Here is my recommendation: get a journal and a pen. Because you are not just going to read passively. You are going to read actively and do your part. There will be exercises and questions to answer. And I need you to play full out. That means committing to reading this book until the end. Pause when required to do the work, and have fun with the process and keep it light.

Treasure Hunter

I have a story for you, and yes, I am starting it with my favorite opening. So here it goes.

Once upon a time, a guy named Mel Fisher believed that there was a treasure to be found deep in the tropical waters of the Florida Keys. It was around 1960. Mel put together a crew and found investors to sponsor him, and he started the search.

Five years later, nothing. Did Mel quit? No. he found new investors (since the previous ones did not want to sponsor him anymore), he got another ship, and he did whatever was needed to hunt the treasure.

Ten years later, still no treasure. He did not quit. He found new bankers. He took different approaches. He created a new plan. He was unstoppable.

Fifteen years later, Mel discovered what he called "The Mother Lode": more than twenty million dollars' worth of gold.

Now you are probably wondering what this has to do with you. It has everything to do with this question: are you a treasure hunter? Do you have what it takes to go after your dream, even if things don't go as planned right away?

You are going to be stretched. You are going to face things that seem insurmountable. You are going to feel despair and stress. You are going to doubt yourself, and you will have to face the people around you questioning you. You will fail. More than once. That is the reality.

Here are the three core beliefs a treasure hunter must have:

1. It exists, it's out there.
2. I will find it.
3. It's worth it.

Let me ask you this: "Are you a treasure hunter?"
Meaning...

- Do you believe without a shadow of a doubt that you will open this new business?
- Will you find a way no matter what?
- Do you know in your heart that this new business will be worth more than anything else to you?

If you answered yes to these questions, then proceed. Embark on this quest with me to find your own personal treasure. Welcome aboard!

CHAPTER 2

I WALKED IN YOUR SHOES

"If you really want to do something, you will find a way. If you don't, you will find an excuse."
– Jim Rohn

Your story was my story. Your fears were my fears. I understand your dream. I know how you feel, knowing deep inside that there is so much more in store for you, that you were destined to make a difference in the world. To create a real impact, even if it was one person at a time. I knew there was so much more for me, and I know you do, too, or you would not have picked up this book. You are at the right place at the right time.

I wrote this book for you to show you what is possible. The key is for you to do your part and to apply what you are going to be learning on this journey. I have thought long and hard about what really made me successful, and this is what this book is about: sharing my personal recipe for success with you! I went from dreaming of living in the USA to living in the USA and becoming an American citizen. From having a job I dreaded to launching my successful coaching practice. From starting my life over twice to being in an amazing relationship and enjoying all aspects of my life. I know what it takes to go after your dreams and make them happen no matter what, even if it seems impossible in the moment.

Where It All Began

I was born in Brussels, Belgium. In the mid-'80s I had the opportunity to spend a year abroad in Texas as an exchange student. I will never forget the feeling I had when I landed at the Dallas airport on that Tuesday afternoon and a wave of intense heat hit me! And then meeting my new American family. They did everything to help me get adjusted to my new life. I barely spoke English when I came here. (Does three years in high school learning English as a third language count?) Now, back then there was no internet, no FaceTime, no picking up your phone and having a conversation with your family whenever it pleased you. Things were very different.

I had decided to make this year the best year of my life. To play full out. And I did just that. My rule back then was, "Say yes to all of the experiences being offered to you (within reason of course), and that will give you an eighty percent win. Create the remaining twenty percent on the spot." It worked, and I had the most fantastic year of my life. So much so that at the end of that year I promised myself I would come back and live in the States forever. I had fallen in love with this beautiful country and all that it represented.

Sure enough, in January of 2000 I did just that: I moved to the States with my husband and our children. I remember landing again in that same airport, this time married with four children, and making sure that our twelve suitcases were accounted for!

I was ready to start a new chapter in our life. Starting from scratch, not just for me but for (and with) a family. This was big. Yet, with clarity, determination, and the right mindset, everything was possible.

The first few years were not easy and were financially challenging. The cost to have kids in preschool or kindergarten was not in our budget. We were not prepared for that cost. Now add to that the fact that I could not legally work because of the immigration process! Nevertheless, our money issues did not stop me from creating the life I wanted. I spent countless hours and resources getting a certification as a life coach. I knew this was part of the next chapter of my life. It was in my heart.

I did not know how (or when) I was going to be able to do it, but I prepared. I did not wait.

Now fast-forward a few years. I had a few coaching clients, and I was starting to make a difference around me. I decided I wanted to get back to a healthier me and enrolled into the Leukemia and Lymphoma Society. They had a program called Team in Training, where you fundraise to donate to cancer research, and in exchange, the program trains you and gets you to the event site, where you participate in your event. I had never run in my entire life, yet I signed up for a marathon.

I had never fundraised, either. I even had to look up that word in the dictionary! But I was unstoppable. I had decided to do it, and I was going to find a way no matter what. Odds were against me: I did not know a lot of people, having just moved to the States, and did not have my own resources to use.

Fast-forward three years later, and I had raised money and participated in seven different events. I wanted to show the world that if I could do it, anyone else could do it too. There was no social media at the time or internet links to use to raise money. It was all handwritten letters sent to friends, friends of friends, and anyone we could think of. I successfully ran a few marathons with them and then decided it was dull to run for that long.

I went on to triathlons, from sprint to half ironman distance, and then finished my journey with a beautiful century bike ride in Lake Tahoe.

How did I do it? The right mindset. Determination. Clarity. Coaches and mentors. Training. In the midst of all this training, I created a healthier version of me. I also became a mentor to other participants and helped them on their journeys to crossing a finish line. The feeling you have when you cross a finish line is priceless. It becomes like an addiction. This is the feeling you will have when you have your first paying coaching client. Trust me!

My Breakthrough

Then life happened for me. I went through a divorce. I remember sitting at my girlfriend's kitchen table, and she asked me, "What do you want to do when you grow up?" and out of nowhere came out, "I want to be a mini Tony Robbins." I remember this vividly. I could see myself transforming lives one at a time, then groups of people, through coaching and speaking events. Totally connected to my life purpose.

This was the beginning of a new chapter for me. Time to start it all over again, this time alone. At that time, the coaching business was not profitable enough to sustain our living needs. I needed to start something fast that would allow me to pay the bills. This was when I started my own remodeling-general contracting business.

Now, I'll spare you the details, but for thirteen years I oversaw my own successful remodeling business. I had created a fantastic team I could really count on. All my work was coming not from traditional marketing strategies, but from word of mouth, the best marketing strategy out there. Everyone's dream! From the outside, it all looked perfect. I was showing up 110% on every job, and people thought I could not live without this job. That this job was it for me. Little did they know I was so unhappy inside. There was this vast void; something was missing. On the exterior, it all looked good but boy, on the inside, I was crying. I wanted out. I did not know how to do it, but one thing was clear: I was done. I had been done for years, but fears kept me from stretching myself and really going after my dream.

We all have our own BS stories...

Now, the funny thing is that I never stopped coaching. I kept the coaching business going somewhat, but the truth is, I could not call it a business as I was not charging my clients. See, when I started as a coach, I was not making enough money. I was taking on clients under the status "pro-bono"! Some were paying, some were not. All I wanted was to coach and I did not focus on the money at all. Big mistake. At that time, I did not realize that I had a fear of asking for money. That I had limiting belief about charging for my services. The underlying cause was really that I did not believe in myself. Who was I to even charge for coaching? There is a name for this: it is called "imposter syndrome." I am sure you are somewhat familiar with this, too.

So, what did I do? Instead of addressing the problem at its core, I went into the remodeling business to create the immediate income needed. And I kept coaching. For free. I knew that coaching was my life purpose, yet I quit on my dream. I came up with the perfect justification for not charging clients for my services: "I was coaching people as part of my own 'religious ministry.'" Such BS. This story served me for years to justify not having the guts to step up and really go after what I loved more than anything else. I did not understand that people need to have skin in the game, that they need to participate in their own rescue using their resources (time and money).

My coach called me on my BS. (You can read this as "BS" or Belief System, your choice.) We worked together on the limiting belief I had, and it was a real breakthrough. At that time, I took a seven day free challenge from Joe Vitale to understand what my beliefs around money were. Joe Vitale is all about creating what he calls "Awakened Millionaires," and watching the videos and doing the exercises really helped me. From there, I worked with my coach on reframing my old story and creating a new story that would serve me more. Once I did the work, I started charging for my services. My coaching business then started growing exponentially.

When people pay you for your services, they are invested in the outcome and the results they are after. When you do not charge for your services, you are either flattering your ego, or you are applying a Band-Aid in that person's life.

There are no long-term results, and yes, you might be planting seeds, but is that really what you want for yourself—planting seeds in others with the hope that one day things will change for them? Or are you ready to step up into your truth and to share your gifts with the world? Or do you have the imposter syndrome and do not believe in your abilities to transform someone's life?

Everything changed for me when I hired that coach and started charging for my services. To this day, I am working with two coaches. One helps me to create results in my life. The other one is a spiritual coach. Our work is focused on spirituality and learning from this lifetime's lessons. Both my coaches are my rocks, that place where I can be vulnerable and totally show up. Where there is no judgment, only truth and growth.

This is what you want to create for yourself. And it starts with you. You cannot expect people to pay you for your services if you are not willing to also do it! It is the Universal Law of

Reflection: everyone around you reflects yourself and your life. Everything that you see is a reflection of you. You notice things in others because you have seen them in yourself first.

I remember one day when my daughter-in-law was disrespectful to me. I could not believe the lack of respect and the words she said to me. We obviously were not on the same page that day and I thought we were working through things. Yet, talking to someone the way she did was beyond my understanding. When she left, I was hurt. I needed to understand. I asked myself, "Where did you not show respect to someone else?" because what we see in others is a reflection of what we have done ourselves. We see it because we are familiar with it. Now, here is the thing: respect is one of the most important values to me. So, I was puzzled there for a moment. What had happened? Until I realized that it wasn't that I was not showing respect to others. No. It was me: I was not respecting myself. I was filling everyone's bucket with love and attention but not filling my own bucket. And I was running from an empty bucket. It was a beautiful lesson.

Ready to Say Yes?

Once I understood the power of the Law of Reflection and really stepped into my own truth, the doors to success opened.

I stopped focusing on my fears of lacking and being stuck. I started focusing on the potential out there and the infinite possibilities that arise from saying *yes* to myself. *Yes* to a successful coaching business. *Yes* to my life purpose.

Enough of playing it small. I realized that every time I say yes, I create the path to achieving my dreams.

Now it is cool to understand this, and when you have the right mindset in place, you can achieve anything you set your mind to! Then it becomes just a question of putting the right strategies in place.

Will you fail? Will some strategies work and some not? Absolutely. Failure is feedback. I started my business without really knowing anything about marketing. I believed that I was clear on how I was to help people. I knew to ask the right questions to trigger answers within them. I knew that we all have answers within us, and it is just a question of reaching for these answers. Was that enough? No.

I originally marketed to people by saying something like, "Hey, you have within you all the tools to be successful. Hire me and I will show you how to use them and will add a few more tools to your toolbox." Well, that did not work. Yet I learned a lot from there. I understood the gap between what I wanted and how I was going about it. I took the feedback seriously. I took new actions and tried new things. And when that did not work, I learned new ways and kept grinding until something really worked.

From there, I created a process. I captured what worked and did not work. Now, through my coaching and process, I have successfully helped numerous clients go after their dreams. One very dear client to me (I am going to name him Jim to respect his privacy) went from being stuck in a job, feeling severely depressed and suicidal, and on top of that going through divorce, to now living every day in a beautiful state, running his own coaching business. Jim is now continually growing, has found the love of his life, and is surrounded by love and blessings everywhere. He had a clear idea of what type of coaching he wanted to do and went about creating just that. Then, of course, life happens *for* you. He started having new opportunities, meeting new people, and from there, gaining more clarity around the type of work he wanted to do with people. He followed the path, and with coaching and guidance, Jim is now living a fulfilling life. He makes a difference in the lives of many people daily and even has a waiting list. Great problem to have!

And this could be you. You can be a success story, too. Now, let me tell you a little about Bill. Bill went from being lost in his life, with no real goals and a job he was not crazy about, to launching his own coaching business. Bill is all about health and mindset. He took the hard path: he had to understand the tools and lessons first for himself. He had to work on his mindset and build that healthy mindset muscle. Some people are faster than others. Some people are more committed than others.

He is now in a successful relationship and has launched his business. His first three clients have had great results in reaching their health goals. Yes, Bill took a longer road, but at the end of the day, he is happy and has learned valuable lessons.

And so will you. You are about to embark on a phenomenal journey and, when you follow the steps, results will be there knocking at your door. At the end of the day, it is your choice.

Enough Is Enough: Can You Feel It?

I remember when the "enough is enough" feeling hit me. When it became urgent to take massive action to go after my dream. To stop playing small and staying in a job that did not give me the fulfillment I was longing for. I already had a coaching certification. Yet, I went for more. I grinded night after night, day after day. Every minute I had available I was studying and growing. I became so focused and determined that it was impossible to not succeed. And I learned so much more about myself in the process. This journey you are about to embark on is your journey of success. Your journey of discovery.

You are going to meet the real you. You are going to understand what you are made of. It is a wonderful journey. And the rewards at the end are high and fulfilling. The feeling you have at the end of a coaching day is priceless. Knowing in your heart that you have helped clients, that you left them in a much better place at the end of a call with you than when they started. Watching them grow into who they were born to be. Crushing their goals. Going after their dreams. You have felt this before, and this is why I am going to show you what it takes to start a successful coaching business. Let's go together after the feeling and knowing that you are living on purpose. Let's get started, shall we?

CHAPTER 3
THE BRIDGE BETWEEN A AND B

"A journey of a thousand miles
must begin with a single step."
– Lao Tzu

W e are going to embark on this journey together where you will learn how to transition from your current job to create the coaching business you want. To go from point A (your job) to point B (your coaching business).

Julie loved helping people. She knew she was born to make an impact in the world. Julie did not know how to go about it. She knew that coaching others gave her fulfillment, yet where to even start? She went ahead and signed up for a coaching certification as well as hired me as a coach.

We worked together for less than a year. Julie was now able to leave her own job and to replace her income with the income coming from her coaching. She had created a recipe for success that works. No longer feeling lost and unfulfilled in her life, she was now full of energy, meeting amazing people and creating the life she always wanted.

Through this book, I will be sharing the same tools and strategies I taught Julie. You will learn how to launch your business while keeping your sanity (somewhat…). Let's be realistic here. It is not going to be a piece of cake, or everyone would do it!

In Chapter 4, you will get clarity on where you are and where you want to be. You will learn how to create breakthroughs in your life. You will have clarity on who you need to be to create a successful coaching career for yourself.

Chapter 5 is about breaking down your outcomes into SMART format while getting clear on what type of coaching you want to do. You are going to want to focus on Chapter 6, as you will understand how emotions do not control us. The power of owning this concept around emotions is going to be life-changing for you. I remember when it clicked for me! The day I realized that no one could make me angry or frustrated and that I was responsible for my own happiness was a game changer.

Now in Chapter 7, it is all about owning who you are and focusing on creating the life you want for yourself and your family. No more barely getting by or just managing your life's circumstances. This is about stepping into your truth and focusing on creating the future you want for yourself. This is about not playing small anymore. I will start to introduce the Reticular Activating System (RAS) and you will learn in Chapter 8 how to reprogram it to get what you want in your life. You will understand the power of using the success cycle and creating from powerful beliefs.

Chapter 8 is slightly different, as you will learn more about manifestation and synchro-destiny.

Chapter 9 contains one of my ultimate recipes to get to the truth of anything happening in your life at any given time. You will have access to three magic questions. Last but not least, you will work on your own recipe for success.

With all this knowledge you will be ready for Chapter 10, where we are going to talk about time management and get some practical tools to be more in control of our time.

Now in Chapter 11, I will talk about the tools that all my very successful clients are using, no matter what is going on in their lives.

And Chapter 12 gets much more practical, as you will get clarity on the steps you need to take to physically get the business off the ground and ready to accept clients!

So, are you getting excited yet? Because I know you are not like everyone. You picked up this book. You are still reading it. That tells me a lot. Put your seatbelt on, get ready, and trust the process. There are no shortcuts. This journey can be joyful and pleasant, or stressful. You are going to decide.

As a coach yourself, I am going to equip you with tools to coach yourself out of negative self-talk and mindset. There will be laughs and tears on this journey. It is like the onion you peel to get to the core of who you are. Don't let the tears and fears stop you. You are going to get clarity on what it is that you are after. What is your core desire? It is never a question of willpower or self-motivation. If you need willpower to achieve something, that means you did not want it in the first place. It's that simple. Fact.

When you have the right desire in your heart, and you have absolute clarity on what you are after, you don't need willpower. You find the motivation to grind day after day. You do everything required to find a way, no matter what.

Together we are going to understand who you need to be at your core to create the success that you want. I am going to share with you how to create breakthroughs in your life. We are going to change the limiting beliefs and stories you have been telling yourself. I know you have them—I did, too. This is why you picked up this particular book. You realized you needed help to get from point A to point B. We are going to do just that together. You are going to do your part. You are going to take notes and do some reflection exercises when instructed, and have fun with the process. I promise you that when you apply what you are going to learn here, you will have the success that you want.

Yes, I will talk about mindset and make sure you create a strong foundation for yourself. I will share strategies and fun tools. I will also go into more of the practical tools needed to open your business.

Now, I have a question for you: do you already have a coaching certification? If yes, great. If no, don't stress. It is essential to get going on obtaining a valid certification. Julian did that while in transition to launching his business. You can get certified as you are learning tools and strategies through reading this book. I will talk more about the various certifications that are out there and the different options you have in Chapter 12.

You are also going to want to start getting clarity around the type of business model you want to set up. Are you going to trade your time for money—many one-on-one coaching sessions—or will you work from a business model where you can decide your own schedule? Perhaps some individual sessions or some days just coaching and other days group coaching? Or having a few programs your clients can go through and then once a week coaching them? There are many possibilities, and I will help you get some clarity around the business model you want to create. We will talk more about this in Chapter 12 when I cover the practical steps.

By the end of this book, your personal toolbox will be full. The bonus here is that you will be able to use these tools again and again. In every area of your life. We are going to set the foundation for success, your own success recipe that you can apply everywhere. Get your notebook, get a pen, and get comfortable. I am ready. Are you?

CHAPTER 4
THE JOURNEY

"The man on top of the mountain didn't fall there."
– Vince Lombardi

You ready? Okay, here is a fundamental question to ask yourself: "Who do I need to be to open this successful coaching business?" Do you need to step up as a leader? Do you need to connect with the part of you that feels confident? That part of you who thinks that you can do anything that you set your mind to?

Who do you need to be?

Breakthroughs

First thing first, breakthroughs. What is your definition of a breakthrough? Right, I know you call it an "ah-ha" moment. I am with you. A breakthrough is really a moment in time when something we thought impossible becomes possible. It is created because of a new conversation, an original thought or idea. Something we read or watched online. Or someone who did something different, and now it's opened doors for others to do the same thing. Here is an example for you: are you familiar with the story of the four-minute mile? In 1954 doctors and physiologists believed that running a mile in under four minutes was impossible. They even thought that you could die from running a mile in under four minutes. Yet, Roger Bannister thought differently. He believed that even if the human body could not normally run the mile in under the four-minute mark, he was the one and only person who could do it. And Roger trained and trained and visualized his victory. Sure enough in 1954, he ran one mile in three minutes and 59.4 seconds. The exciting part is that once he opened the door to that extraordinary performance at the time, forty-six days later his record was broken. And to this day, we have over 36,000 high school kids who are running under a four-minute mile. This example shows that a breakthrough can be created by a new belief, a new way to look at things. Sometimes when someone else has a breakthrough, it then creates breakthroughs for yourself.

What is a breakthrough you have had in the past, in your personal life or in your professional life? What happened? How did it come about? Go ahead, grab that journal again, and take some notes. (Now go write! You will thank me later!)

Did you stop and write? Okay. You know, success leaves clues! And if you are serious about creating more breakthroughs in your life, you must know your own recipe.

Now, here is a shortcut for you: there are three keys to creating a breakthrough.

Are you ready? The first key is your emotional state, the second your story, and the third your strategies. In the coaching community, we call that "state, story, strategy" in that order.

Here is the truth: everyone goes for the strategy first, the "how." "How am I going to do this or that?" And I bet you've asked yourself more than once, "How am I going to open my new coaching business?" And then...you probably created a story. Maybe something like, "I am stuck at my job, it is never going to work." You might even have persuaded yourself that you do not have what it takes to open your own business. Or you are buying into the story well-intentioned people around you created for you. A limiting story. And now, your emotional state is probably frustrated, anxious, impatient...and I can keep going here. Are you with me so far?

I have news for you: "How" is always available! Ask Google! If you are serious about creating a breakthrough in your life, you must start with the question, "Who?" Now, watch this: write "how" on a piece of paper. Then shuffle the letters, and you obtain "who." Pretty cool, right? And this is the key, right there. Ask yourself, "*Who* do I need to be to open that coaching business I have been dreaming of for so long now?"

So, who do you need to be? Do you need to let the confident part of you take charge? Do you need to make the leader part of you show up? Because the truth is, we play so many roles within us.

You know what I am talking about. That part of you that is anxious. Or depressed. Or angry. Or impatient. Or the other parts of you that are more empowering like joyful, happy, peaceful, etc.

I am getting carried away here. Can you tell just how much I am passionate about this concept? This is the key to achieve anything you want in your life. It all starts with the right mindset. But bear with me: you will read all about this in Chapter 6.

Going back to creating your breakthrough here. I shared with you that it is always your emotional state first. Then, when you are stepping into the right part of you—let's say the confident part—then from that place, you can create a better story. What would your story be when you feel confident about opening your coaching business? Think about it for a moment. Is it something like, "I always find a way"? "I know that this is part of my mission in life, and I am unstoppable"? How does it feel now with this new story? Yes, you can smile.

Lastly is the strategy. You have the emotional state, and you have the right story in place. From here, you will be able to find the approach needed to open your coaching business, all because the right part of you is in charge. Through this book, I will cover these three keys in more details.

You and I, we are going to spend some time on mindset and gaining clarity. Then we will go more into the stories and really understanding which ones are serving you and which ones are not. Finally, we will talk all about strategies.

I know. You are waiting for the procedures! That's part of how we have all been raised! At a very young age, you started asking questions that all started with how: "How do I tie my shoe, Mom?" And then later on, you are all about how: "how

I am going to get this business started?" "How am I going to make it happen?"

Okay, I get it! Time to go to the next chapter!

CHAPTER 5

CLARITY IS KEY

*"Clarity precedes mastery and the more clear you can
get on what you want to create in your life, the more
focused you will be in your daily behaviors."*
– Robin Sharma

So, here we are! You love helping people. You know you were born to make an impact in the world, and you wonder where to even start! Together, we are going to get some clarity. The first thing that comes to mind is, what are your "riffs"?

By riffs I mean the various topics that you could talk about for ten, fifteen, twenty minutes, passionately with no notes at all. These are your favorite things in the world to share or to teach. Take ten minutes right now to think about this! Pull out your journal and write your top five or six riff topics. (Now go write! You will thank me later!)

The second thing that comes to mind is, where have you had the most success in the past? What kind of results have you achieved for yourself or your friends in the past? What are the things that you have worked on or helped people with, that came so naturally to you?

I remember my coach asked me that same question when I was struggling to figure out a niche for my own coaching. At the time it was a lightbulb moment for me: relationships and divorce prevention! I had been coaching and helping so many people around relationships, and helping couples create a strong foundation in their relationship that it became a no brainer: I was to become a Divorce Prevention Coach!

So, for you, what comes naturally? Where have you had great results in the past? Again, pull out your journal and do some thinking time here around that. (Now go write! You will thank me later!)

You want to have your own coaching business. There are a lot of different schools of thought about having a niche or not. My take is to follow your intuition on that. You can go very broad, or you can specialize yourself. And let's be honest: by now you probably know what the coaching you want to do is about! You are thinking, maybe fitness or health. Or even mindset. Or perhaps, relationships, or business and corporate coaching. You know in your heart what really talks to you. Follow your heart!

As you are going through your coaching certification you will gain a lot more clarity. By doing the exercises around the riffs and the results you can get for yourself and for others, you will have even more clarity. I personally started really broad as it was all about mindset and sharing tools and strategies. That did not really work out. When I started my coaching business, I had the idea that we all have the tools within us to be successful and to have a fulfilled life. That was way too vague, not really clear enough for the client to understand what was in it for him. I made the mistake of falling in love with the name I had created for my coaching business, MyLifeToolBox. I assumed (big mistake) that just reading the name would give total clarity to the clients. It was obvious, no? Not so much!

Then I went more specific as shared earlier and focused on Divorce Prevention Coaching. A few years later, after going through an intensive worldwide coaching academy, being trained by the best to be the best, I created Results Now Coaching. This is more about helping clients to get the results they want in their personal and professional lives.

My point is, you want to connect with what really resonates with you. Get back to those riff topics you wrote. Get back to the results you have had in the past. That's where you want to start.

You Are the Pilot

Before we get carried away with your planning here, let's make sure you are sure what coaching is about. I am going to use a metaphor here to help you be on the same page. Let's say that you are getting in a car with your client and he sets a destination in the GPS. Your client is the driver of the car. For a minute, imagine that you have decided to drive to Los Angeles. You, as the coach, are the co-pilot. As co-pilot, you will make sure that the destination reads 1234 Sunset Boulevard Los

Angeles, California. You will make sure that your client, the pilot, knows precisely the destination. (Side note here: yes, you can change the target if you wish to do so!)

Here is the key. Your client is the pilot. He decides how fast he is going to drive, if he will be stopping, and if he will be taking the highway or the side roads. He is in charge. He does the work. Now you, as the co-pilot/coach, are going to look five percent in the rearview mirror. This means checking for these limiting beliefs that might come up. Let the client know about the blind spots. Tell him about what you see that he doesn't, because he is focused on the road. As the coach, you will keep him accountable for the distance he said he was going to cover that day. Ultimately, he does the work while you support him. That simple. You follow me there?

Coaching is not therapy. It is not counseling. It is not mentoring.

Coaching is asking the right questions to trigger the correct answers that are already within your client. Coaching is setting up some accountability and letting your client know about the things that you see but they don't because they are in the middle of it!

Coaching is creating a non-judgmental space for your client to grow and bridge the gap between where he is and where he wants to go. Remember, coaches do not diagnose. Coaching is focused on the present and future, not the past. Coaches can help maximize performance and accept people where they are and guide them to move forward. That's a pretty good summary right there!

As a coach, you'll need to become an expert at using these metaphors and even finding your own way to explain to someone else what coaching is. Because you will hear that question often!

Are you still with me? And did I mention that as a coach you are not your client's friend? Don't cross that line or there will no more coaching possible. You have to set boundaries from the beginning of the client/coach relationship. Can you relate to how your coach—under the umbrella of rapport—tells you what you need to hear, even if it hurts?

Let me say this again, since it is essential: as a coach you are not your client's friend. Period.

SMART format

Okay! Are you ready to get a little deeper here? Let's do it! It is crucial to understand where you are right now to get clarity about your present job situation. And from there you can decide where you want to go. Now the key here is to use the SMART format: Specific, Measurable, Actionable, Realistic, and Time defined.

Remember the driving example? Saying you wanted to get to Los Angeles would have been way too vague! But "1234 Sunset Boulevard, Los Angeles, California" is much better! The result you are after needs to be very specific. You need to be able to measure it, it needs to be realistic, and it needs to be something that you can take action on. You also need to be very specific about the time. "A few months from now" is not clear enough. A clearly defined day, month and year is key.

Go ahead, grab your journal and write down what your SMART goal is. By what date do you want to open your coaching business? It should read something like this:

"By October 1st, 2019, I will open a successful coaching business." Notice here that we did not say "within three months" or "in ninety days." No. We are specific. We are "time defined." And you can even add a few feel-good words (e.g., successful).

I remember when I learned the SMART concept! I was blown away by how much most of us mix up actions and results. For example, if a client says to me, "I want to run four times a week," that goal is really an action, not a result. As a coach I will ask something like, "What will you get from running four times a week?" And I will most likely hear something like, "I want to lose weight" or, "I want to be ready to run a marathon next year." Can you see the difference between actions and results?

I will then help the client write the result they want into a SMART format. Here, using our previous example, it would look like, "Lose ten pounds by October 30, 2019." One of the actions the client will take is to run four times a week.

Clarity Tool

Take a deep breath. Smile, you are getting ready to get even more clarity! Okay, let's do it. Here is a fantastic tool that is designed to get you laser-focused on the direction you want to go to. You first must start with your current status, where you are. What is your starting point? Perhaps you hate your job, or you want to get healthier, or you are not too sure of your existing relationship. Maybe you are ready to make an impact on the world. Write that down. All changes start with complete honesty. You might feel uncomfortable in certain areas of your life, and this exercise will expose that. And that is okay. This will feel like ripping a Band-Aid off and exposing the wound. And then you touch the wound, and it causes pain. And pains cause movement and change. So, let's do this. Let's get clear!

Pick up that journal again. We're going to start with, "Where are you?" The truth, your current situation. What are the pain points? Why do you want to quit your job? To start your own coaching business? Do you want to make more money? Do you want more time for your family? Do you want more time for you? Do you want to live your life purpose? Do you want more fulfillment?

I recall doing this exercise with my client Teresa. She was living with her parents and she never had enough money. She had way too much month left after her paycheck was spent. She was not fulfilled in her underpaid job and all she wanted was to move out of her parents' home and start living her own life. She was thirty-four at the time, and she knew that it was time for things to change, as she had finally touched rock bottom. It required her to be transparent and honest with herself to realize that her situation was not sustainable and something had to change.

Now, your turn. Write your truth. Be transparent! This is the starting point.

1. Write down your current situation and circumstances.

Where are you, and what is your current situation?

2. Now, let's figure out where do you want to go. Play along here. Project yourself a year from now. Let's say that right now it's October 2019. Project yourself to October 2020.

In your mind's eye, project yourself in the future. It is one year from today, and this was the best year of your life. What did it look like? Look back and start writing down what the best year of your life looks like!

Once you are clear on what your best year looks like, you need to go deeper.

3. Project yourself two years from now. It is now October 2021. You look back again and this time, it was even better than your best year ever. Describe what happened. Get creative. Go into details.

What does it look like now? What do you have more of? More time for you? More family time? More revenue? More clients? More fulfillment?

Whatever it is, what does the top best year of your life look like?

Start writing it down and then when you are done, smile! Because, my friend, this is the juice! It is what you are going to focus on. It will give you wings. You know where you are going!

Did you do this exercise? Did you go ahead and write in your journal? Do it. Stop reading right now and go for it. (You will thank me later!)

And by the way, here is another truth for you: most of the time when I ask one of my clients what they want in life, well, they feel stuck and they start by telling me what they don't want.

So often people get sucked into what they don't want out of life. They can tell you, "I don't want my job," "I don't want to feel stress anymore," or "I don't want to work for this boss anymore." Yet when I ask, "Where do you want to go? What are you after?" I usually get answers like, "Good question, I am not sure. Let me think about it!"

What, Why, How

Have you heard the expression "you are in the rat race"? I call that "running on the treadmill of life." We don't stop. We are busy running on this treadmill, expecting to get somewhere. And be honest here: it is not working! Therefore, you are here reading this book. Ready to create a change. Ready to go after your dream. Ready to step up the game. It is vital to get clarity on what it is you are after. To find the fuel within you. To connect with your heart's desire! Because at the end of the day, it is never a question of motivation. It is a question of having the right desire in your heart. When you have the right desire, you will find a way. You will make the time. You will be unstoppable.

Now you are wondering, where is she going with this? Patience, I am getting there.

It is never about "how" I am going to do this. "How am I going to open this coaching business while paying the bills?" It is about getting clear on the real outcome you are after. The "what." The result you want for yourself. (You know now to write that outcome in a SMART format.)

The next step is to focus on the "why." You just did the exercise on getting clarity about what your best year looks like to really connect to what is important to you.

You have to find the right leverage. What is going to give you the fire in your belly? What will keep you up at night and make you impatient to get up in the morning? Leverage is super important. Leverage is linked to either pain or pleasure. And leverage needs to be immediate. Think about someone overweight. The doctor tells that person that if she continues like this, a few years from now she will have serious health issues. Do you think that she will change her behaviors? Probably not. Now if the doctor tells her that the way she is going she probably has two more months to live, you bet she is going to make drastic changes. When you create leverage, you must create a sense of urgency. For example, if you know that you only have two months of cashflow to pay the bills and that you have to launch your business as soon as possible, you will find a way.

We also call this "burning the boats and taking on the island." If you would quit your job right now, with two months of cashflow, that would be burning the boats. There is no turning back. You can only move forward and make it happen. You have find the right leverage for you that will get you moving forward. People will do more for others than they would do for themselves. Meaning that if you cannot find leverage, think about who is going to be impacted by your results. Once you have launched your business, will you be more flexible in your schedules? Are you going to pick up your kid from school instead of having him in an aftercare program? How will that feel?

Will you be less stressed, and how will that benefit your relationship with your spouse? Can that be leverage right there?

Here are five questions for you to find your leverage:

1. How will this feel?
2. What will this mean?
3. Who do I become on this journey?
4. What is the pain of not achieving my goal?
5. What is the pleasure of succeeding?

Take a few minutes here in your journal and connect with the reasons why it is important for you to succeed and to launch your new career. Feel it in your bones. In your guts. Feel the emotions behind your reasons. Give it a good cry if needed, get to the truth. You will thank me later!

Now, once you are clear on your "what" and your "why," it is time to write the MAP. This is your Massive Action Plan. This is where you are going to do a brain dump. Write down all the things that you can think of that you need to do to get that coaching business open. Write everything that comes to mind. Don't judge the thoughts, don't analyze the ideas. Just write the thoughts as they come.

From there, you will write a plan. You will decide on which actions to do first. You will schedule these—what gets scheduled gets done. And from there you will be able to measure your progress, because what doesn't get measured, doesn't change. So, you are going to check off one item at a time. You are going to revisit your plan weekly. Possibly daily.

There was a fascinating study conducted at the Dominican University of California. Researchers took a group of people from various business and organizations and they assigned the participants randomly to five different groups.

The first group was asked to think about the goals they wanted to achieve in a four-week period and to rank them by importance and difficulty.

Group 2 was instructed to do the same but to also write their goals on paper and to rate them.

Group 3 had to do all that Group 2 did, but was also asked to write an action plan for each goal. Now you see where I am going here, right?

Group 4 did all that Group 3 had to do, and was asked to share their goals and actions commitments with a friend.

Group 5 went all in by doing all of what the other groups were doing and on top of that, they had to send a detailed weekly report of their progress to that friend.

Now at the end of the study, forty-three percent of participants in Group 1 completed their goals, compared to seventy-six percent of participants in Group 5 who achieved their goals.

You got it? It is key to get clear on your goals! The results you want! And to fuel it with leverage. And then to write the massive action plan. No "but's" or "if"s"...do it!

So yes! Time to get crystal clear on the what, the why, and the how. How is your MAP—Massive Action Plan. Once you have a MAP, you will want to schedule the various tasks and actions. And then you are going to measure your progress… again and again.

CHAPTER 6

WHO DO YOU NEED TO BE?

*"If you sit around waiting for what you're wanting
to find you, the only thing you'll discover is that
it didn't find you while you were sitting around
waiting. You are in charge of how you're showing
up in every moment. Any perceived exception to
this truth is an illusion. Knowing this is bliss..."*
— **Michael Nitti**

Okay, I have talked quite a lot about clarity in the previous chapter. Now it is time to go even deeper and to look at the practical stuff. Don't be an ostrich: stop burying your head. You must know exactly where you are at financially. Money. This word is often linked to many fears.

FEAR is False Evidence Appearing Real. Or do you prefer F* Everything And Run? Because that is so often what we all do. When fear kicks in, we avoid the difficult conversations. We don't take the next step. We freeze. We ignore. We play it safe. We find excuses for why it is not going to work. We have a long list of these.

And because we don't look at the facts, our brain goes and fills the gap with fiction. You know what I am talking about here. Think of your reaction when you are sending a text message on your iPhone or on Facebook Messenger. You sent the message, and now you see those three little dots. It means someone is answering, right? Yet suddenly the three dots stop. And what do you do? You think to yourself, "Maybe I should not have sent that message." Or, "Perhaps they are too busy to talk to me." Or, "Maybe they are upset at me." Or, "I can see how I am not a priority here." Blah, blah, blah. Right?

We all do this! Our brains, to protect us, will create fiction when there is a gap in information. Here the facts are "The person did not answer." The fiction is the stories you tell yourself.

Okay, going back to the financial situation: are you clear on exactly how much money is coming in and how much needs to go out every month to pay the bills? How much money do you need to bring in before you can let go of your current job? If you let go of the real job before launching the coaching business, how many months' worth of savings do you have to cover bills? What is the bottom line here? Sam, another one of my dear clients, was so sure he knew exactly what his financial situation was. Until, he put it all on paper! That was the wake-up call he needed. What he thought were the numbers, was far from what the real numbers were! Once he put together a budget, and then went back and tracked the last two months of expenses, he knew exactly why he could not get out of the mess he was in. That is were it all starts: you have to look at what the truth is, no matter what.

Remember what I shared earlier? You must know where you are starting. What is the financial picture? Go ahead. Grab your journal and write down where you are at financially. Get the budget out. Check the bank statements and get absolute clarity to the dollar amount on your financial picture. (Do it now. You will thank me later.)

The Power of Emotions

Okay. You are back. Let's keep moving forward. Now, I bet you might be feeling a little uneasy. Perhaps you feel better because you understand your financial starting point. Perhaps you feel a little stressed. Or even you might feel impatient and worried. You might have a disbelief that you are ever going to find a way to quit that job of yours and find a way to open your own business! You might have dreamed about it for so long now, and yet it seems so far away. I hear you. I have been there.

I started in 2004 as a coach. And then life happened *for* me. Because, my friend, life happens *for* us, not to us. I had to start another business to make money fast to pay bills. I started at the bottom of the ladder as a painter. As the years went by, I learned, I stretched myself, I went from one formation to another. I followed people who were successful and had been there before. I was in "grinding" mode!

Fast-forward ten years or so later. I am a successful general contractor and interior designer. I have a successful business, and my monthly income is really sweet. Can't complain. Now it is funny how things work out: all these homeowners that I worked with, I always ended up coaching them, coaching someone in their family, or one of their friends. I still had my business, MyLifeToolBox. It was not a successful coaching business at that point, but through the remodeling business I had tons of opportunities to coach.

You can probably relate. The idea of starting your own coaching business perhaps came about because you find yourself coaching people around you left and right. The remodeling business was very profitable. Yet, it was not enough. Fulfillment was not there. Passion was not there. I can tell you what *was* there: Stress. Tons of pressure. Sleepless nights. It took me quite a few years to really make a leap of faith and decide to go full on with the coaching business and to start charging a decent price for my services.

The truth is, I was miserable. I was so good at my job that everyone thought that it was what I would be doing for the rest of my life. And on the outside, I would smile. And cry inside. My heart was aching. I was dreaming of the day I would not have to work in that business anymore. I was even picturing myself dancing while drinking champagne to celebrate that I had finally quit that job! Yes, I was miserable, stressed, and let's be transparent here, very unhappy. I bet you understand and relate.

If you find yourself in a similar place, and you realize the emotions you are feeling daily are disempowering emotions, the first step is to ask yourself, "What else do I want to feel right now?"

Maybe the answer is happy. Perhaps it is creative. Maybe it is confident that you are going to find a way to get out of that job of yours.

The second step, once you know the emotion you want to feel, is you are going to ask yourself, "When was a time that I felt that emotion?"

Let's say you want to feel confident.

When was the last time you felt confident?

What was happening at that time?

What were you doing?

What were you thinking?

What were you focusing on?

What can you do now to bring back that feeling of confidence right now in your life?

This is a great exercise, and I am inviting you once again to take your journal and start writing.

Here are some key questions to take control of your emotions.

Ask yourself, "What I am feeling right now?"

Then ask yourself, "What else do I want to feel?"

Next, "When was the last time I felt this way [the feeling you want to feel]?"

"What do I need to focus on right now to feel this way again?"

Are you writing? Go write! Do this exercise. (You will thank me later!)

Is This an Expression of Who You Are?

Okay, you are back! Mindfulness and presence are essential. You know, when you feel stuck in a disempowering emotion, you need to ask yourself this magic question: "Is this an expression of who I know I am?"

You might come across very tense and unapproachable to some people, or you might feel very anxious. Yet, is that really who you are at your core? Is this really an expression of who you know you are?

Observe when something shows up. Check in on the mental story and/or the emotions. What is the feedback you are getting? The feedback helps you make a choice on what is next.

As you imagine it in your mind's eye, check again how it feels and decide what is next. If you get a "Yes, I like what is next," then great. If you get a no, then make an adjustment by asking again, "Is it an expression of who I know I am?"

Even better here, ask this one: "Is this an expression of who I know I am and want to share with the world?" If yes, great. If no, modify your story. Check the energy of the emotions showing up.

Remember, you are contributing to this exact moment. You want to have this moment-to-moment awareness. When you actively engage, your life will become a life of fulfillment. When you are ever-present, you can choose and decide how to react and to respond. Reacting is emotional. Responding is deliberate.

At the end of the day, there are a lot of different emotions out there. We have over two thousand words in the English language to express our feelings. Yet we have probably no more than twelve emotions we feel daily. We experience the same emotions day after day. Like, if you think about it, you pretty much see the same clothes in the wash weekly and you eat the same meals over a one- or two-week period. I will talk about this more in a later chapter.

First, I want to share a fantastic formula around this.

You Are in Charge of Your Results!

Please write this formula in your journal. Here we go:

Event + Response = Results.

It is like 1 + 2 = 3. Right?

You have an event happening.

You respond to the event.

Now you have a specific result.

For example, you have a conversation with your spouse about you quitting your job and opening your coaching business.

You realize your spouse is not supportive of your idea.

Now you have a choice of how you are going to respond.

Are you going to fight over this with him? Are you going to ignore his input? Are you going to listen to him and thus forget about your dream?

What will your response be? Because the truth is, it's your response that will give you the result.

The key is to turn the formula around. 1 + 2 = 3 becomes 1 = 3 - X. The key is, what is X?

Event = Result. And then we decide on the response!

Let's go back to the example.

Event: you have the quitting conversation with your spouse.

The result you want is to ultimately quit your job and open your new business.

What do you think your response to your spouse's objections needs to be?

Will your responses be from a place where you feel defensive? Or from a place of love and open communication?

Always focus on the result that you want first and then pick your answer.

Okay, here is another example I can share with you. Imagine that the event is that hubby is frustrated and he snapped at you when he came home.

You can respond by snapping back.

The result is then probably a very tense evening together, if even.

Now, go back to the start: hubby is frustrated and he snapped at you.

The result you want is to have a lovely peaceful evening together.

What will your response be? I bet you will not snap back. Got it?

Remember that at the end of the day, what is wrong is always available, but so is what is right. What are you going to focus on?

Are you going to focus on what is right; what is going to allow you to move forward?

Are you going to focus on how overwhelmed you are, such as, "There is so much to do before opening the business"? Or are you going to focus on every step, every simple action you can take every day and, by doing so, the progress you make?

By the way, grab your journal and write down this golden nugget I just gave you.

"What is wrong is always available, so is what is right." (You will thank me later!)

CHAPTER 7

CREATOR OF YOUR LIFE

"Once we realize the extraordinary power we have to compose our lives, we'll move from passive, conditioned thinking to being co-creators of our fate."
– Jason Silva

I have a compelling question for you.

Are you a manager of your life circumstances, or are you the unstoppable creator of your life?

Another golden nugget alert here! Make sure to capture this question in your journal. Now, you wonder, what is she talking about here? A manager versus a creator?

The 80/20 Pareto Principle

Do you remember I spoke earlier about the breakthrough concept? Well, let's go deeper. You have noticed by now that I am talking a lot about mindset stuff. Here is the reason. Success is eighty percent mindset and twenty percent strategy. (Journal alert: write 80/20 in it!)

Newsflash: to open your business, the recipe for success is eighty percent mindset and twenty percent strategy. No "but's" about it. Fact. This relates to the Pareto Principle. This principle states that, for many events, roughly eighty percent of the effects come from twenty percent of the causes. Like in life, eighty percent of your results come from twenty percent of your efforts. Or eighty percent of your business comes from twenty percent of your clients.

You see this principle everywhere. Here too. 80/20 is the key to success. It's that simple. Now, going back to our breakthrough concept: remember, it starts with your emotional state. And you must ask yourself the critical question, "Who do I need to be?"

Let me teach you something that will create a breakthrough right now for you! Here it is. Ready? We *do* emotions! Yes, you read this correctly. I used the word *do*.

This was a real breakthrough for me when I was introduced to this concept. I remember feeling like everything in life was happening to me and that I had no control over my emotions. Like the weather happens to us and we can't control if it is going to shine or to rain! The day I understood that emotions are not like the weather and that I had a say over the emotions I was feeling in every instant, my life changed for the better.

Emotions don't just happen to us. No one can make us mad or angry or happy. We feel a certain way because of our physiology, what we focus on or believe in a given time, and what words we are using at that moment.

It is not like you are walking down the street and suddenly you step in a puddle of water and anger starts falling from the sky on your shoulders. It does not work that way!

We *do* emotions. Think about it for a moment: if I say to you that someone is sitting in a Starbucks somewhere in the world right now and that guy seems to be very depressed, and I asked you to describe the guy, you could do it. You will tell me that his shoulders are slouched, that he is not smiling, that his head is low, his breathing is shallow, and he is not looking at anyone. And you could probably go on with even more details. Perhaps this sounds way too familiar to you…

Now think of a person born blind. Yet, when this person is happy or anxious, or frustrated or joyful, you see it right away in their posture. Right? This blind person has never seen anyone's physiology before. Like they have not "seen" someone being happy or angry. Yet, they know precisely what the physiology of each emotion is. Why is that?

Because it is in our DNA. We *do* emotions. The key here is to understand that there are three patterns to every emotion.

Your posture or physiology is the first pattern you can control to change a feeling. Your brain knows the physiology of each emotion precisely. Think of our example of the depressed person. You knew exactly what that guy at Starbucks looked like. You know the physiology of someone happy, or confident, or anxious.

The second pattern is your focus, your beliefs. What you focus on you will feel. What you believe about a situation or a person or about yourself will determine which emotion you will feel. For example, if you think that no matter what, you always find a way, that you are unstoppable, or that you are knowledgeable and ready for the next step, you will definitely feel confident. But if you focus on what you don't have or on what is wrong right now, or you focus on your fears, and on all the steps that you need to take to open the business, you will probably feel anxious and overwhelmed.

The third pattern is your language, the words that you are using in every given moment. If you go about life saying life is hard, you bet life will be hard! Because the words that we speak give us the experience we have.

If you argue with your spouse and then refer to the argument by telling your friend something like, "He stabbed me in the back with that idea," I promise you that you will feel very different than if you say something like, "That idea really left me somewhat puzzled!"

Your words have incredible power. Change your words, and you will change the emotion you have at that moment.

Can you think of a moment where you felt angry about something? And then the phone rang. And you picked up, and the person on the line had no idea that you were mad. Couldn't even tell. Why? Because you changed your focus right there. You changed your physiology, and you used different words.

Now I have another classic example for you: you might be screaming at your kids, and the phone rings. And the other person can't tell since you are having a perfect—joyful even—conversation. Then you hang up the phone, and you go back at it with the kids because they still have not done what you asked them to do. Can you relate?

The key to understand is that no one can make you feel a certain way. You feel that way because of what you are focusing on at that precise moment. Because of your body language at that moment. Because of the words you are using.

This is magic. Golden, to say the least. Now you can decide in every moment, "Who do I need to be?" To open your business, is it the part of you that feels insecure and anxious that needs to show up or is it the part of you that feels confident? What is your own recipe for being confident?

Okay, time again to pick up your journal.

Let's use the emotion of being confident for this exercise.

First line, write "physiology."

Second line, write "focus and beliefs."

Third line, write "language and words."

Now write down what you do, focus on, and say to yourself when you are confident. Do it. Now. You will thank me later.

Here is my recipe for the emotion "confidence."

Physiology: shoulders back, strong on my two feet, balanced, direct eye contact, smile, slow breath, and certainty in tone of voice. Talk not too quickly, not too slowly. Just right. Sense of commanding the room, the space.

Focus and Beliefs: I will find a way no matter what. I am unstoppable, I am knowledgeable. People trust me. I have what it takes in this moment. I can do anything I set my mind to. I have faith and God has my back. It is already a done deal.

Language and Words: I got this! Let's do it! I am ready! Bring it on!

Note that everything I used in the pattern "focus and beliefs" could be used in the pattern "language and words." I could have, in that last pattern, something like, "I am enough, I am knowledgeable, I can do this, I have faith, etc."

When I write in the third pattern, I think about what I say to myself just before walking into a meeting. I got this! I am ready, etc.

Great, here is the next step: as I shared with you earlier, there are different parts within you representing mixed emotions. Like the confident part, the fearful part, the joyful one, the one that is the lover, and so on…so many different ones. Each of them has their own secret recipe. You want to capture these.

Do you know how to get a dog to come to you? You call him by his name! Right? Same here! You want to name these different parts of you. Because they each must show up when needed and you want to be able to call on them.

Write the recipe and then name that particular emotion with a fun nickname! In my coaching practice, this is one of the first exercises I get my clients to do. We write together the recipe for the emotion they need to step into to achieve a particular result. And then we name it. Let me tell you, I am working with Gladiators, James Bond, Lions, Cougars, Tom, and so on!

There are no rules to naming that part of you. Have fun with it! It can be a nickname, or the name of someone you would refer to as confident, or an animal, or even a superhero. Your pick! Do not overthink it, just do it. Because this part of you that is confident, that's the part that is opening the new business!

So, you have a name for the part of you that needs to show up! Now you want to create a list of options. This is what I mean here. When you are not feeling confident, what are the things that you could do right away to change your physiology? To change your focus? To change your internal dialogue?

Maybe you could have a picture on your phone that shows you being confident. Perhaps you could go to the closest bathroom and scream your heart out. Or maybe you are in a building with stairs, and you can go up and down the stairs a few times for no reason other than changing your physiology and thus, how you feel in that instant.

What else could you focus on? What about writing down three things you are grateful for that day? Can you see how that would make a big difference in how you feel?

Pick up that journal again. Come up with a menu of options you can pick from to do a quick change of emotions on demand! (Trust me, you will thank me later!)

When I need to step into confidence, I first ask myself, "What would RockStar do right now? What would she say?" (Yes, that is one of my confidence's name!)

If these questions are not enough, I then go up and down the stairs three times, for no other reason than to change my physiology. Or I turn the music on very loud and sing my heart out (when surroundings permit). Or I do three jumping jacks. Whatever it takes to change my physiology! And of course I change my internal dialogue and start focusing on the things I can control or directly influence.

Your turn. Put a menu of options together to help you change your emotion on demand!

Reticular Activating System (RAS)

Remember how I talked earlier about how you are the unstoppable creator of your life? You create your experience with your thoughts. Many books explain this concept well, so I will not bore you with it. Yet let's talk about the RAS—Reticular Activating System—for a minute.

This is important to understand as you can learn to reprogram your mindset to achieve your goals. Our RAS focuses on whatever is occupying our thoughts at any given moment. For example, do you remember the last time you bought a car, and then suddenly you started seeing that same car everywhere? Or the time your best friend told you she was pregnant and the next thing you noticed was pregnant women everywhere?

I have a question for you: can you feel the fabric of your clothes on your legs right now? Yes? Yet you did not feel it a few minutes, ago right? The explanation is simple: your RAS says, "Okay, this is her focus, let me focus on that too." Let me show her all the opportunities around by looking through the endless bits of information that surround us every day until I find something that fits that reality. It is straightforward. What you focus on you will find more of.

When you think, "I am terrible at remembering names," your RAS will respond by failing to focus on people's names. Now you can recalibrate your RAS by concentrating on more positive thoughts, and it will reprogram itself to see opportunities where it once used to see only negative situations. If you start thinking, "I am amazing at remembering names," your RAS will focus on names more and help you remember them.

When you are using positive and affirmative wording, your subconscious mind will align with that, and you will be well on your way to creating that new reality. I could do hours of teaching around this, as it is fascinating.

A critical thing you need to remember is that your subconscious does not know the difference between what is real and what is not. When you speak in affirmative sentences, your RAS will align and show you all the possibilities around you. It will open doors to the infinite wisdom that is already within you but had yet to be shown to you.

It is vital to understand that you need to take control of what you want and to learn to not negotiate with your mind. Your mind will play tricks on you. Let's talk about this for a minute.

Picture this scenario: It is the evening, and you decide that tomorrow you will get up at six a.m. (while you usually wake at seven a.m.). The alarm goes off, and your brain says, "Just stay one more minute" or, "Are you sure you need to get up now?" etc. Can you relate? It comes up with so many excuses and reasons why not to get up. This is when you will need to take control of your brain. Pardon my French here but this is one of my favorite expressions for you to start using: "Make your brain your slave!" Yep, that's right. You are in control, not your brain. And when your mind starts negotiating with you, you need to take control and say "enough," and then immediately do the action that you had all good intentions to do in the first place.

Why am I sharing this with you? Because you want to take charge. There will be lots of various thoughts and fears showing up as you figure out the next steps to launch your new business.

You want to step up in your truth and follow your dream and not get distracted by all the thoughts that will show up as your brain is trying to protect you.

Success Cycle

Remember, your mind is running this old software whose job is to protect you at all costs. This brings us to the following vital information you need to understand. When you have a limiting belief that, "It is going to be hard and I don't have what it takes" you will see a limited potential to succeed. From that place, you will take minimum actions and therefore have minimum results, if any, and it will reinforce your initial belief that yes, "It is going to be hard and I don't have what it takes."

Now imagine that you step into the part of you that is confident. And from there, you create the belief that, "I will find a way no matter what." You will see every opportunity around you as potential. You will be taking massive action. By doing so, you will now have great results. This will reinforce your belief that, "I will find a way no matter what!"

At the end of the day, your mindset is everything! The beliefs you have, the internal dialogues you create and listen to, the part of you that shows up at any given time.

I am going back to the initial question opening this chapter: are you a manager of your life circumstances, or are you an unstoppable creator of your life? What is it going to be for you?

CHAPTER 8

YOU ARE NOT ALONE

"Where focus goes, energy flows."
– Tony Robbins

When was the last time you manifested something critical to you? You really wanted that one thing? Can you recall a moment like that?

I remember manifesting my dream of living in the States. This was some twenty years ago. The day my family and I took the plane to fly from our native country, Belgium, to Texas, USA, was a big day for us. We were accomplishing a big dream. We had made it happen! I had lived for that day for quite a few years. I knew in my heart it was going to happen one day. Now, this was a big step: imagine flying across the continent with twelve suitcases and four kids to start your life all over again in a different language and different country.

I am going to share with you the secret ingredients to my success recipe to manifest anything I set my mind to. By the end of this chapter you will be in a great position to manifest anything you want in your own life!

Three Levels of Manifestation

Let's go back for a moment to my special day, January 11, 2000—the day we flew to America once and for all. Because here is the thing: as much as I was happy and excited, at the same time my heart was crying as I was leaving behind my best friend, my soul sister. As we took off that day, I remember promising myself that one day I would fly back, rent a car, and show up at her doorstep unannounced.

Two years later, I did just that. See, there are three levels of manifesting anything you want in your life. Level One is when you have an affirmation about your heart's desire. You can focus on that every day and keep repeating it to yourself. This Level One is more like an affirmation. You say or write something over and over. You do not really attach emotions to it, it is really just a sentence describing what you are after. "One day I will meet my soulmate" or, "One day, I will have a successful coaching business." It is something that you say to others. You might not even believe it yourself just yet.

Now Level Two is going to look like this: "One day I will have a successful coaching business. I can already see my practice being full. I will be helping clients every day to get the results they want. I can't wait." Here you are more detailed, and you attach emotions to the desire that you want to manifest. You have more certainty and you can already feel it in your guts. Like, yes, I am doing this, watch me. I got this!

The key is to play the manifestation game at Level Three. And Level Three is what I did when I manifested living in the States. Years before that, I would see myself moving into the new house. I would be taking the kids to school and spending time with my new friends. I could feel the Texas heat just thinking about it and I would close my eyes and see the blue skies.

Here is an example of what Level Three looks like (side note, here you are on the phone with your best friend):

"Joan, you are not going to believe this! I launched this new program yesterday, and I already have five clients who have signed up for it. I was so excited yesterday when one of my clients had this massive breakthrough. By the way, I forgot to mention to you that I found the perfect color to put on my office's back wall and when you see it next week, you are going to love it. I signed for that program called Zoom and now I can coach all over the world using this virtual room. I love it!"

Can you see the difference? In Level Three, you step into the moment like it is a done deal. You have already accomplished what you desired in the first place. It has happened. You are stepping into the moment, and you link it to powerful emotions and to all your senses. That's the key here!

Going back to flying back to Belgium, getting a rental car, showing up on my best friend's doorstep…well, I did it so many times before in my thoughts. Again and again. I knew all the details. I saw myself getting that rental car, driving on the specific roads that would take me to her house. So many times. I saw in my mind's eye the look of surprise on her face when I showed up on her doorstep. I felt the embrace as we ran into each other's arms. I saw myself wiping the tears of joy that were rolling down my face. I could taste the coffee she was going to make within minutes of us getting together.

That is the power of manifesting at a Level Three. And you can do it too.

Don't think of your new business as something nice to have one day. Talk about it like it is a done deal. See yourself in it, coaching your clients. Get very specific with the details.

Remember, at the end of the day, your RAS does not know if something is real or not! Its job is to protect you by deleting information all around you at any given time. Yet, the minute you see, feel, and experience yourself having achieved a goal, your RAS will make sure to open all doors and show you every single opportunity available to make the manifestation you were stepping into in that moment your reality.

Incantations

Are you ready to add some turbo to manifesting? Okay, here it is!

With motion, we create emotions. When you take an affirmation, and you repeat it repeatedly, it will have a very different impact when you add emotions to it and you engage your physiology. Tony Robbins calls this an incantation. Here is a fair definition of an incantation: "an incantation is a phrase or language pattern that is said out loud and with an actively engaged physiology."

Empowering emotions have unmatched power to inspire the certainty and the emotional intensity that you need in order to create anything you want in your life. Like, you don't just go to the gym a few times and hope your muscles will stay in shape. Your muscles need to be kept in condition. Same goes for your emotions and beliefs: they must be trained to be in peak performance condition.

When you use incantations, you are really using the three patterns of creating an emotion we talked about in Chapter 7. By creating new patterns of language, physiology, and focus/beliefs, you are creating a new cause-and-effect direction and destination for your life.

In more practical terms, this is where you repeat the affirmation, yet you engage your physiology, your body. You create movement. You feel it in all the fibers of your being. You are standing up and engaged. And you feel the empowering and positive words that you are saying. Again and again. Repetition is key.

Note that in our Level Two and Three manifestations we included emotions. Using incantations is the secret to manifesting your desires even faster.

A few months ago, I went to several high-level training and immersion events, one after another, and did not spend as much time working on my coaching business as I would normally do. I was not stressed about it, as I had a plan. I created a powerful incantation. "I attract a minimum of four new clients by the end of this month. *Yes!*" I would sing it in my shower. In my car. I would repeat it, being totally engaged with all my senses, several times a day for ten minutes or so each time. The more I would use these incantations, the more I would feel empowered, and it felt like a done deal. There was no doubt in my mind. Fast-forward a month later, and I had four more clients in my book of business. That's the power of an incantation!

Here are a few examples of incantations:

I am abundant and prosperous, yes!

I love my life, and I am so blessed.

Every day in every way, I am getting better and better!

I bring massive value to my clients and facilitate breakthroughs!

I attract the right people, the right circumstances, resources, and opportunities that will allow me to launch a successful coaching business by December 2019.

Okay, you know the next step by now. Pick up your journal and write down a few powerful incantations of your own. (Yes, you will thank me later!)

Formula to Manifest

Did you do it? Okay. Time to dive even deeper into manifestation. Here is the formula to manifest.

Clarity + Alignment + Actions = Manifestation

Another mentor of mine, Christie Whitman, explains this well in her book *The Art of Having it All*. Great resource!

You must be clear about what you want, what you are after. At the same time, you want to maintain a state of allowing where there is no resistance. This is vital.

A state where it feels good, you are at peace, you know you are going to find a way no matter what, and you feel excited and happy with what is right now in the present moment.

Once you are clear about what you want and you are in this state of allowing it to come to you, you are opening doors for more to come into your life and to manifest what you truly desire.

When you have too much clarity and are not aligned, you will feel angry and frustrated. Probably some irritation, also.

When you have too much alignment and not enough clarity, you will find yourself depressed, bored; the results are slow to come, and you might find yourself resigned.

Taking actions when you are not clear or not aligned is exhausting. You will find yourself pushing through. On the contrary, when aligned and clear, you will feel the pull.

The key is to have enough clarity and alignment to create anything you truly want. Alignment is really surrendering and relaxing about it. Not being tense. Not focusing on what is not working.

As I shared earlier, one of my favorite sayings is, "What is wrong is always available, and so is what's right." (Golden nugget alert here!) When you align, you are focusing on what is working, and you are taking the next step and then the next one.

Can you relate to a time where perhaps you wanted to release five pounds before the summer? You could see yourself in that cute swimming suit? You are on the beach sipping on a cocktail, and you feel fantastic and terrific in your own body? This is clarity.

Now if your internal dialogue goes something like, "It never works, I always do yo-yo weight, I look awful in my clothes, I have tried everything and nothing works" you would be sabotaging yourself and you would not be aligned. Positive internal dialogue is essential.

We have worked in an earlier chapter on getting clear about what you want around the new business. Now connect to what it is going to feel like to have that business. Connect with your emotions to make sure that the energy you are putting out there is aligned with your outcome of having a new business. From that place of clarity and alignment, you can take massive action.

I believe I am the queen of manifesting what I want in life! I have done it again and again. From creating the life I wanted here in the States, to a successful remodeling business, to launching my own coaching business, and, last but not least, getting my dream home. And did I mention attracting the guy of my dreams? (That is another story for later!) And all this by directly applying the various principles I covered earlier.

Synchro-Destiny

Not overwhelmed yet by all the tools I am sharing? Great, because here is another one! It is called synchro-destiny! My friend and Coach Michael Nitti shared this concept and a version of this exercise with me. Once you step into the energy of creating your dream, of opening your new business, and you truly align yourself with your truth, you are opening yourself to synchro-destiny: things start to happen, opportunities appear out of nowhere. You meet the right person at the right time, who allows you to go to the next step. You stumble across an article online that gives you an answer you have been looking for a while, etc. This is where the magic happens! All because you are focusing on the results you are after and you are allowing it to happen.

Yes, you guessed right. Pick up your journal! Now it is that time again to get some self-reflection going. You are doing this exercise because success leaves clues, and it is vital to open yourself to all possibilities. Pick up your pen and start writing. (You will thank me later!)

Please answer the following questions:

1. What is something that showed up in the past in your life by pure coincidence, yet you followed up and it led to something meaningful?

    Did you then take action? What results did you got from taking action?

    Were you happy with the result you obtained, or did you push further to bring it to an even higher level?

2. Think of a time where something showed up as a coincidence, and you just watched it but did not follow up on it.

    What actions could you have taken and where do you think it might have led you?

    What do you think your life would look like if you had followed and taken advantage of what the Universe had sent you?

Be open to the synchro-destiny in your life; it is there, all around you. Look for it. Open your eyes to the infinite possibilities and the magic of it. When you do so, it will become like an addiction. You are going to want more of it!

CHAPTER 9

CHANGE YOUR STORY, CHANGE YOUR LIFE

*"Change your story, change your life. Divorce the story
of limitation and marry the story of the truth and
everything changes."*
– Tony Robbins

A re you with me? Ready to go even deeper? Remember the onion metaphor I shared with you earlier? You have done a lot of work so far, peeling back one layer after another, getting to the core, the truth of who you are.

From this place of truth, everything becomes possible. From this place, you will be opening your new business and figuring out a way to success. At the end of the day, remember it is not really about the destination, it is about who you become on the journey to success.

The Work

This brings me to something important for you to start working on, because let's be honest: there will be fear, limiting beliefs, and disempowering thoughts that will show up. The question is: what do you do with that? Simple. You are going to question those beliefs and ideas. Katie Byron has a unique process called "The Work."

Observe the thoughts that show up. Ask yourself, "Is this the truth?" and observe what answers you are getting. Go deeper and ask yourself, "Is this really the truth?" and note what else shows up. This will bring you back into your heart and out of your head.

Now my two favorite questions are when you ask yourself:

"Who would I be without that thought?" and

"What would I do differently if that thought was not there?"

I remember one weekend sitting outside on the back patio, excited to be finally having a phone conversation with my husband, who was out of town.

The facts were that I had been traveling a lot, I was finally home, and my husband had to leave to be with his parents for the weekend before I came back. They really needed him, as they were in crisis mode. So here I was, Sunday morning, enjoying a morning coffee and dialing my hubby's number. Not two minutes into our conversation he said to me, "Honey, I got to go, Mom is doing crazy stuff in the kitchen." I was like, "Just wait, you'll get to her in a few minutes."

Sure enough, no, he had to go right then. "Bye, honey," I heard, and…click.

I went straight into thinking about how I was "obviously not his number one priority." I was upset. And then the magic question came in: "Is that the truth?" Well…okay, I am not his priority…today. The truth is I am his priority other times.

Yet, what is really the truth here? The truth is, this weekend was not about me but about being there for his parents! This is really the truth. The truth is we can connect later. The truth is he would be back soon, and then we would have all the time in the world.

Who would I be without that thought? The old me would have been pretty upset all day at my husband.

These questions are powerful, and they bring you back to facts, to what is really going on, not the fiction and stories you create in your mind. I then turned my state around. Who would I be? Well, I decided I was going to be someone who was going to take the day for herself and not worry about anyone else! I had a fantastic day, went to lunch with a friend, took a nap, and got myself a pedicure! All that because of a couple of magic questions!

The truth is you can stick to a story, you can focus on what is wrong, you can focus on your fears and marry your limiting beliefs. Or you can turn those beliefs around, focus on what is right, and create a new story. What is it going to be for you?

Remember when I shared the difference between facts and fiction? Your mind always wants to protect you. And in the absence of facts, your brain will create its own fiction. The more you focus on the fictions, the more they will become your new reality, and you will even add more and more details to them. The next thing you know will be this story you created that is far from the truth. When using the turnaround questions, you will free yourself for stories, and you will be able to go back to your heart.

Now, when you doubt yourself when limiting beliefs show up, or even when someone says something to you, go ahead and use these questions. This is the quickest way to get back to the truth of what really is.

Only from the truth can you grow and progress. Only from the truth can you create your new coaching business and have the guts to move forward no matter what!

What else can you do with these limiting beliefs? Here is a six-step process.

Take one at a time and ask yourself:

Step 1: What is the limited belief I want to work on right now?

Step 2: What emotions are showing up when I have this belief?

Step 3: What actions am I taking or not taking when I have this belief?

Step 4: What actions would I be taking if that belief was not there?

Step 5: By taking these actions what new emotions do I now have?

The final step, Step 6, from this place of taking further actions and feeling new emotions is: What is the new belief I must have? *Et voila!*

Here is an example for you.

Step 1: Limiting Belief: "I will never be a successful coach."

Step 2: Emotions Showing Up: depression, failure, overwhelm, stuck, procrastination, and frustration.

Step 3: Actions: really, no actions. A lot of procrastination and making excuses, keeping myself busy with other things. Most of them unrelated to creating success for myself.

Step 4: If the Belief Was Not There: I would be learning marketing tools; I would talk to other successful coaches and study their success; I would hire a coach for myself; I would grind; I would smile; and I would take massive actions in any and every way possible.

Step 5: Now the New Emotions Are: confidence, leadership, success, empowerment, certainty, and control.

Step 6: From the Step 4 Actions and Step 5 Emotions the new belief I am creating is: "I am a successful coach!"

Your turn! Pick a limiting belief and turn it around. Go ahead, grab your pen and start writing! You will thank me later.

Are you done? Okay, let's go back to what your truth is for a moment. You have had success in your life in the past, in small ways and in significant ways. Think about it. Yes, you guessed it right: take the journal out again, as you are going to create your own recipe for success.

Here is what I would suggest you do:

Go into the past and look at different moments in time where you felt successful.

What did it require?

I often see in a recipe for success things such as:

"I prayed, and I knew a higher power had my back."

"I had faith."

"I did not quit."

"I focused every day and measured my progress."

"I scheduled my tasks."

"I told my coach about what I wanted and created some accountability."

"I had a plan."

"I had absolute clarity on what I wanted."

"I made it a must, not an option or nice to have."

Etc.

What is your own recipe for success? Go ahead, write—you will thank me later!

CHAPTER 10

YOUR PERSONAL
LIFE TOOLBOX

"Gratitude will shift you to a higher frequency,
and you will attract much better things."
– Rhonda Byrne

We have covered a lot of tools and strategies for you to fill your own personal toolbox. Yes, you already have a lot of answers within you and a lot of tools. All you need to be successful is right there within you. At any time, you can reach for the tools that are going to get you to move forward. Are you ready for more? Because I have a few more tools that will make a significant difference.

Will It Make the Boat Go Faster?

Here is my magic question for you: "Will it make the boat go faster?" Okay, I know you just read that sentence a second time wondering, "Where is she going with that?"

This simple tool will help you make better choices around your decisions, keeping you focused on the ones that will get you a step closer to opening a new business. With every decision, no matter how small or big they are, you must get into the habit of asking yourself that simple question.

This question makes the difference between coming in last and winning at the highest level. Back in 1996, a British Olympic rowing team came close to last place in the Atlanta Olympics. Four years later, in the Sydney Olympics, they won the gold medal. Why? Because before undertaking any action, as a team and individually, they decided to always ask this vital question: "Will it make the boat go faster?"

As an example, "Will extra training make the boat go faster?" Yes.

"Will going out on Saturday night make the boat go faster?" No.

You want to keep asking yourself this crucial question. Every action you are about to take, do a quick check first.

"Will stepping into doubt and focusing on my limiting beliefs make the boat go faster?" No.

"Will watching two hours of TV make the boat go faster?" No.

"Will working on the new coaching program's specifics make the boat go faster?" Yes.

You get the gist of it. My point is, use it! It will create magic in your life!

Suitcase 168 by 52

Now there are so many actions and decisions you can take at any time. Many things continually require your attention. Between taking care of the household and the kiddos, keeping husband happy, performing in your current job while doing everything you can to launch your new business…it is nonstop.

I hear you. I have been there. One thing that made a difference for me was becoming an expert at time management.

The first thing I am going to say here is that it is never a lack of time or a problem of time management. It is always a question of having the right desire in your heart. Think about it for a moment: when there is something you absolutely want, you find a way to make the time for it.

Same concept here: you want to transition to that new business and get those first clients. You have absolute clarity around that. The next question is not, "How am I going to find the time to do this?" but more, "Where am I spending my time now?" Again, clarity around where your time is being spent is critical.

Here is one of my favorite metaphors for you: At birth, you were given a suitcase. The dimensions of this suitcase are 168 by 52. You and everyone else in the world got the same suitcase. The question is, what do you put in it? See, there is only one resource in the world that is fair for everyone: the resource called time.

52 weeks. 168 hours in a week. We all get the same amount of time; the question is what we do with it! Now here is what you are going to want to do next. Grab your journal and create what I call your draft suitcase. You know how before going on a trip you might run a mental checklist of all the things you want to pack in your suitcase? Here you can do something similar. Think about where your time goes every week. Perhaps you sleep seven hours a night: this is a block of forty-nine hours going into your suitcase. You might be spending forty hours at work, ten hours at the gym, fifteen hours with the kids, and so on. You get the picture here. What does your draft suitcase look like?

Once you are done with this exercise, commit to tracking where you really spend your time for the next seven days, starting tomorrow morning.

Seven days from now, you will be able to compare your draft to the real suitcase, and I promise you that it will probably be a wake-up call.

You are going to find hours that you did not know you had! Every time you have the thought, "I don't have enough time to launch my new business," you can go back to this exercise. Because I promise you, you absolutely have time!

Once you have the data for your real suitcase, you are going to divide the stuff you have in there into four categories.

Category One, called "Distraction," is going to be what you spend time on that is "not important and not urgent." E.g., social media or binge TV watching.

Category Two, called "Delusion," is going to be "not important but urgent": here are those moments when you are working on something or busy with something, and you continuously interrupt yourself to answer the demands of others. Like you might be having a nice lunch with the family and then the phone rings, and you interrupt yourself to answer the call. Or you might be a slave to your email inbox or even a slave to your phone. Think about how whatever you are doing in that moment, you just stop to answer texts, emails, or phone calls.

Category Three, called "Demand," is "very important and urgent." This is what I call "Life." This is the phone call you get because your kid got hurt at school and you need to go straight to the hospital. You drop everything, and you go. You answer the demand now. For example, a colleague is sick, and you do their work to meet some deadlines.

Category Four is called "The Zone." Here it is "very important but not urgent." This is where you want to spend at least fifty percent of your time. This is fulfillment. This is where you focus on what is truly important to you, but it is not urgent. For example, exercising is important to you, but it does not matter if you go on Monday morning or Monday night.

Now, go back to your real suitcase (seven days from now). And look at your various activities daily: where do you spend your time? Are you living in Distraction and Delusion? How much do you answer to Demand? How much are you really in The Zone, cruising and feeling fulfilled?

The Not-To-Do List

You are going to use this real suitcase that you are putting together, for one more thing: seven days from now, you are going to create a "Not-To-Do List." Yes, you read that right. Not-To-Do List. (Again, you will thank me later!)

Take the actions you are doing on a weekly or daily basis. Sort them into three sections: automate, eliminate, and delegate.

Automate. What are the tasks that you do that could definitely be automated? Are you still writing checks and mailing them, or are you doing it online in less than fifteen minutes a week? What about at work? What can be automated? Are you scheduling appointments manually, or are you using a booking system that updates your calendar accordingly?

Eliminate. What are the things you spend way too much time on that really need to go? Honesty here is vital. Social media? Do you tell yourself "I can take ten minutes to check my business page" and the next thing you know, one hour later you are still checking everyone's posts? Time to eliminate that.

Delegate. This is where you are going to buy back your time. This concept is phenomenal. Let's talk about it for a minute.

Suppose you are spending six hours per week cleaning the house.

Now, you could hire someone to do that for you. Depending on where you live, you are looking at around a $200 cost for someone to clean your home. Yet, if you use these six hours to do an income-producing activity, you will have a huge ROI— Return On Investment—or ROT—Return On Time.

During these six hours, you could be creating your next marketing campaign, or doing some strategy sessions and enrolling clients into your new coaching program. Just bringing one client into your coaching program will bring you in a lot more than the original $200 spent on the cleaning lady.

You get the point here. Continually finding ways to buy back your time will make all the difference in your life. And yes, I know you can clean or do the groceries or cut the grass or do the laundry.

Who else could do these tasks for you so that you can focus on what is really going to make the boat go faster? Bringing in these first clients? Getting a step closer to launching your new business?

Prioritize

And if this Not-To-Do list is not enough for you, here is another strategy that is going to give you even more clarity on what to spend your time on. You ready?

Get your journal out and complete the sentence, "I know I am successful when…"

When do you know you are successful? Think about it for a minute. My list looks like this:

"I know I am successful when I can travel anywhere in the world, anytime. When my kids need me, and I can support them in whatever way they need—time, money, or anything else. When I am making an impact through my work and facilitating breakthroughs. When I am empowering people to become who they were born to be. When money is not a showstopper. When I spend time with my family."

I have many more insights around, "how do I know when I am successful." Just with what I shared, you can see that I value freedom, contribution, love, connection, and growth.

Your turn. Go ahead and write down what your rules are for being successful.

You will thank me later.

Okay, you are done with this first part. Here is Part Two of this exercise.

Go back to your real suitcase and look at what you spend your time on. Make a list of the main projects and activities you do weekly.

Take each one of them separately and, on a scale of one to five, five being the highest, rate that activity according to the following three criteria:

1. Is this an income-producing activity?
2. How much fulfillment does this activity give me?
3. How much is this activity aligned with the values I uncovered in the "I am" success exercise (Part One)?

The next step is to add your results per activity. The sum is really the priority number for that activity in your life. It is ranking the events by order of importance. Doing this exercise will allow you to get clear on what needs to go and what can stay! How cool is that? Do this exercise, you will thank me later!

The 4 Ps

Are you going to still use "not enough time" as an excuse? Can't do that anymore! You just got quite a few fantastic tools to add to your personal toolbox.

From this place where you know you have time to create the life and the business you desire, it is vital to use another strategy. I call this one the 4 Ps.

P stands for Plan, Prep, Prepare, and Persevere.

You plan your week, you prep for your week, you prepare your week, and you persevere no matter what! Let's take an example around health.

Imagine for a second that you are on this health journey and have decided to go into conscious and healthy eating.

On Sunday, you would Plan the food, the menus for the week, and your grocery list.

Then you would Prep the food you just bought and get it ready to go for the week. That means cleaning the veggies, cooking some already, and separating them into portions ready to be used during the week.

Now the key is to Prepare. Prepare means that even if you have a plan, and you have "prepped" the food for every day, there will be things happening during the week that you cannot foresee on Sunday! Maybe on Wednesday your boss invites everyone to lunch! (A girl can dream, right?) You want to be ready for that eventuality by knowing in advance what you will be ordering at the restaurant. You want to know in advance how you are going to handle any out of the ordinary situation that might arise. It is like having a Plan B.

Persevere tells it all. No matter what, you are not going to quit. You have a bad day? You make a terrible choice? Okay. Reset the next morning. Go at it again. Step into your state of confidence you created earlier in this book and get back to it, no matter what.

The same can be apply for to your transition here. You have a Plan for what you need to accomplish in a given week. You are going to Prep for it, like making sure you are blocking out the required time and getting all the resources aligned so that you can progress. You are going to Prepare, meaning having a Plan B if something comes up on Tuesday so you can make it up the next day. And no matter what, you are going to keep moving forward. Persevere! Because you've got this! Remember the visualization exercise you did earlier in this book, when you manifest in the third dimension, like it is a done deal? Get back to it, and I promise you it will fuel your heart and get you moving again!

Twin Voices: Angel and Devil

Now, it is a fact that you will hear different voices inside your head. This is how I see it: you have on one shoulder the procrastination devil and on the other shoulder, the progress angel. It goes like this: The angel is saying something like, "You are doing an amazing job, I am proud of you, look at how much you have accomplished this week."

Now the devil is saying something like, "You are doing an amazing job, you have accomplished so much this week that it is now time to stop and go have fun. You don't need to work so hard. And how do you even know you are going to succeed? Maybe you should just quit for now." Can you relate?

This is what you need to do to take control of these internal dialogues: capture them! Write the conversation in two different colors. One for the angel and one for the devil. Then read it back out loud using two different voices. This will take all the power away, getting you out of your head and back into your heart. It is powerful. Just know that the procrastination devil will get bigger and bigger the more you feed him, meaning every time you are procrastinating and finding excuses, he grows.

The other way around works too: every time you say, "No, I am not going to listen to you, I am moving forward and working on this one thing right now," he gets weaker and weaker. At the end of the day, you decide which voice you are going to listen to!

Take a breath! I gave you many strategies in this chapter! Yet, one more is to come. This is probably the most important of this entire book. Are you ready?

It is...Hold on! I am not just going to give it away like that.

Here is the question: What is the antidote for anger, frustration, impatience, overwhelm, procrastination, anxiety, and depression, this rainbow of emotions that you are probably feeling at one point or another as you are on this journey?

Okay, here it is. The antidote is...gratitude. Gratitude! This is key to remember.

The minute you change your focus to what you are grateful for, everything changes. It is the special ingredient that will get you going no matter what. Gratitude gets you moving forward.

When you are feeling a disempowering emotion, the quickest way to change your focus is to find one thing right there that you can be thankful for.

Imagine if you had on your desk a clear jar filled with colorful sticky notes. Every time you have a win, you feel grateful for the progress you have made in getting your business a step closer, you have learned a new tool, you had a great conversation with a potential client, and so on, write it down on a colored sticky note and put it in the clear jar. Right there for you to see every day! By doing so, you are stacking the wins, and creating more wins. Gratitude all around.

CHAPTER 11
RECIPE FOR SUCCESS

"The body doesn't know the difference between an experience and a thought. You can literally change your biology, neuro-circuitry, chemistry, hormones, and genes, simply by having an inner event."
— **Dr. Joe Dispenza**

"**N**ot my circus, not my monkeys!" I don't know who said that, but I love that expression. Make this sentence part of your vocabulary. Because there will be so many things distracting you, requesting your attention, pulling you in different ways. And you are going to have to decide if these things are your monkeys and if they belong to your circus. You have enough on your plate! Time to protect yourself and be a little selfish.

I have two keywords for you, "Heck Yes!" You want to check with yourself when someone makes a request of you to do something, to participate in an event, to do them a favor. To drop everything and come to this one thing that means the world to them.

The Power of Rituals

Do a gut check. If you do not get a "heck yes," then it is *no*. Simply no. Build that discipline to say no and to protect yourself. You are going to need it over the next few months as you grind and do whatever it takes to create this new business.

Discipline is really a key word here. I have explained earlier in this book the importance of time management, right? Now the key is to be disciplined. No matter what is coming your way, you stick to the numbers of hours per week you committed to working on setting up your new business.

You keep using the tools the tools and strategies I have shared in this book along the way. It is not enough to be aware of your emotional state once. You need to check in with yourself more than once a day, again and again.

And the critical sentence, "Is this going to make the boat go faster?" Not a one-time deal either. Create your own recipe for success: what do you commit to doing daily that will help you be in the right emotional state and get you moving forward?

Rituals are essential. I can tell you this: in my coaching practice, I know which clients are going to be successful and achieve their results faster and which are not.

The clients who show up to every call prepared, do the work in between the coaching sessions, and have rituals in place, these are the ones who get the results they are after. Understanding the importance of the investment they made in themselves and having absolute clarity on the results they are after makes the difference between getting results or not. They are willing to do the work no matter what. And they show up daily for themselves. They have no excuses when the alarm goes on in the morning. They use that first hour in the morning as their hour of power. Some meditate, some do a priming exercise. Some exercise first thing and others write in their gratitude journals. Some ask themselves the night before, "What are the three things that I need to focus on tomorrow? What are the three actions that I can take tomorrow to get a step closer to my goals?"

Non-Negotiable

The successful ones, they have a recipe for success. They have rituals in place, and they know what the non-negotiables are. Okay, now you are wondering what non-negotiables are! Here is some clarity for you: do you ask yourself when you wake up in the morning something like, "Is today a good day to do crack cocaine?" Probably not. Because to you, the thought doesn't even cross your mind. It is not something you wonder about. It is non-negotiable in the sense that it is something you don't do. No second thoughts around it.

Or another example: do you ask yourself in the morning, "Is this a good day to brush my teeth?" That thought does not cross your mind. Because again, it is non-negotiable. It is part of what you do every day.

You want to come up with your own list of non-negotiables. What are the things that are part of who you are? You don't need to negotiate with your mind. It is part of you, like taking a shower or brushing your teeth, or wearing clothes to go to work.

You guessed it, it's time to take your journal and write a list of what your non-negotiables are.

What are some that you want to create for yourself as part of your recipe for success? Like, non-negotiable: writing ten things I am grateful for in my journal every day. Or exercising every morning for thirty minutes. Or perhaps, meditating every day. Or doing some breathing exercises. Whatever you come up with, it is your list, and it needs to work for you.

You can find a lot of resources (just ask Google!) about that first hour in the morning and how powerful it is! Tony Robbins created an exercise called "priming." It works wonders. Basically, after some sets of breathing, you spend a few minutes in gratitude. Then you have another few minutes working with the energy and grounding yourself and, last but not least, you spend three to five minutes future pacing yourself. This means you step into the future version of yourself, where you see yourself having reached your goals. It is a done deal. (Remember the manifestation in three levels? This is where Level Three comes into play.)

Successful people prime every day, no matter what. It is non-negotiable. Give it a try. You will see the impact it has on your emotional state and on your day in general. You will become unstoppable. Last year in November, after reviewing my finances and knowing what was to come in December, I decided that to finish the year on a high note I needed to create an extra $5k of income. Just like that. So, in my priming exercise every morning, I would see myself looking at my bank account and seeing the extra $5k. It was a done deal. No doubts. Not buts. I did this over and over again. Sure enough, fast-forward to the end of December and I had a little over an extra $5k in the bank!

I also used this concept with my client Paul. One of his goals was to bring in an extra $2k per month so that eventually he would be able to cover for some of his parents' expenses. We created solid incantations together and we changed the limiting belief that all he could bring home per month was $10k. See, here is the thing: you have a financial ceiling. In Paul's example, he knew that no matter what he would bring in $10k every month and that all the bills would be paid. Sometimes he did not know how, but he just knew that every month it all would work out. His financial ceiling was $10k. Together, we increased that financial ceiling to a minimum of $12k per month. He had to focus on the same feeling of certainty he had for the $10k to now be $12k. In his priming, he saw himself checking his bank account and getting the extra money. He saw himself giving a check to his parents to cover their mortgage. He primed and pictured that, day after day. Sure enough, a few months later, he had raised his financial ceiling and started paying for his parents! Do you have a financial ceiling? What is the amount for you that you know without a shadow of a doubt will come in every month no matter what is going on? You don't really know how but you know that the bills will get paid. What would happen if you raised your financial ceiling?

What is that new number you are going for? Please write it down in your journal! You will thank me later.

Part of this recipe for success is to be accountable. You must have an accountability system in place. A coach. You are about to open your own business, and how can you get clients to believe in you and trust you if you are not willing to do yourself what you are asking them to do?

Everything changed for me the day I decided to hire myself a coach. I had been in business for a while and was not attracting the clients I wanted. The day I hired a coach, I started drawing in more clients. That simple. I was doing myself what I was asking my prospects to do: hire a coach.

Time for another metaphor: can you picture the Winter Olympics ice skating event? Picture the beautiful couples in the ice rink doing incredible steps and dancing so in sync. They look perfect to you, right? The truth is it took them countless hours of practicing, of falling and getting up, or adjusting their techniques. Of going at it one more time. And then one more again. And working with and trusting their coach.

As you picture this couple, with your mind's eye see on the side their coach watching their every move. Taking notes. Does the coach look like he could even make all the dance moves the couple is doing on the ice rink? Probably not. Because he does not need to. He needs to be on the side and have a 360º view. To see what the couple cannot, as they are in the middle of the skating rink.

This is what a coach does: sees what you can't see yourself as you are on your journey. Helps you make that two-millimeter shift that will make all the difference at the end.

If you were flying from Dallas to Los Angeles and only looked at the compass just before getting there, the wind could make you end up in Seattle! Yet if along the way you keep checking the compass and adjusting as needed, one millimeter here and another here, you will get to your destination.

This brings me to another favorite question of mine: "When is *now* a good time to start?" *Now*.

Time to pull out your favorite journal, as this next chapter is about the practical steps you need to take to open your business. Get ready!

CHAPTER 12

PRACTICAL STEPS

*"When the need to succeed is as bad as the
need to breathe, then you'll be successful."*
– Eric Thomas

Remember the formula for success? 80/20. Eighty percent is the mindset, and twenty percent is the strategy. I gave you a lot of mindset tools to get you to the finish line faster. Time to get to the meat and get clear on the practical steps you need to take to open your business.

Disclosure statement here: In this chapter, I will be sharing with you some of the services that I use myself. I have no affiliations with them or benefit from sharing these with you. I just know that I love the services I am currently using in my own business. You must find the ones that are going to work for you.

The first thing you need to ask yourself is under what name will you be conducting the business? Will you be using your own name, or will you use a more specific name?

Like when I started as a coach, I used the name MyLifeToolBox.

I thought it perfectly represented what the business was about: the tools that you need to go about your own life. This name came from the idea that we have all the tools we need within us. Sometimes we need to be reminded of them, or we need to add more tools to our own toolbox. With that idea in mind, MyLifeToolBox was born.

What is the name that you want to use that represents something to you and can be easily linked to your new business?

Your next step is to figure out a separate phone number! Trust me on this one. You want to have a number that is dedicated to your business. You want to set up business hours as well. I have no problem admitting to carrying two cell phones, one personal phone for friends and family and one for my coaching clients. The latter stays in my office on weekends and at the end of the day. I have set boundaries for myself. I have a private life, and I respect that. For myself and for my family.

Do the same starting immediately. I used to have only one phone. When it was ringing, I never knew if it was a client or someone else. And that created a lot of chaos in my personal life.

My clients know that I do not answer the phone after hours. They can send me a text, and I will get to it when I can. Between you and me, I do check my work phone during the weekend, maybe once or twice. It is at my discretion. And if I want to address the text, then so be it. Otherwise it is for Monday to deal with.

Now you have a name and a business phone number. Time to start thinking about what your official mailing address will be. Will you be using your home address? Or perhaps a P.O. Box?

Will you share a co-working space and use their address? With the digital age we live in, you do not need a brick and mortar business. All you need is a good internet connection, a computer, and a phone. Minimum investment. Possibly a link to a co-working space where you can use a private office as needed (if you are meeting a client face-to-face, this is more professional than a Starbucks or your personal home).

Now that you have these essential elements in place, it is time to go official. You want to check the legislation in your own state. Some states request a business license. Not all do. Also, decide if you are going with a DBA—Doing Business As—or an LLC—Limited Liability Company. Again, you need to check with an attorney what the best solution will be for you. I personally started as a DBA for a few years, and as the coaching practice grew, I opened an LLC to protect my personal assets and my family's.

Take a breath. Here comes the next step. Go online and apply for an EIN number. It is an Employer Identification Number, a nine-digit number assigned by the IRS. Very easy to do. (Ask Google how to do it.) This is to allow the government to track your gains. You will need this number to file your business tax return! Take the business name information, the address, and the DBA or LLC paperwork together with the

EIN number and get to a bank of your choice. Ask to open a business checking account. And voila! You are officially in business!

Now you want to start making all the expenses related to your business from that business account. Do not mix your personal expenses with the ones for the company. That would be very messy. Start keeping every single receipt. You will thank me later when you do your income tax next year! Look into hiring an accountant.

Or you can even start and use your own program to track expenses, invoices, and so on. I personally use FreshBooks to keep track of every transaction, in or out. Some people like QuickBooks. And there are many other programs out there. You need to decide what works for you. Then my CPA files my taxes once a year. Easy peasy!

Take another breath. You did all the official stuff. Now it is time to do the internal stuff.

First step: create a contract. When a client signs up with you for X months of coaching or X sessions, you want to have an agreement between the both of you. You can draft a contract, or you can ask an attorney to do that for you.

Look into DocuSign or other similar digital programs that allow you to email the agreement to the client and do everything electronically.

Okay. You have your first coaching client who just signed the contract. Now you need to have a way for your clients to make a payment. There are many options. PayPal is a classic one. Or you can sign up for a service that allows you to take credit cards. I personally use Stripe and have never had an issue with them.

There are upsides and downsides to pretty much every service out there. You want to do your own due diligence and find what is going to work for you. Be aware of hidden costs and fees.

There are two more steps I would recommend you put in place.

The first one is to make sure you are using a calendar system. There are many different ones out there. Pick one. Schedule Once? Time Trade? Suite pocket? And so on. Again, ask Google! Do your research. I use Schedule Once as it is so user-friendly and easy to set up. The cost is minimal, and you can personalize it to fit with your branding. I tried Time Trade and it was too complicated for my taste. I like low cost, user-friendly, and professional!

These digital calendars will integrate with a general Google calendar so that all your personal and professional stuff is on one screen. I use different colors for different events. Remember when I shared that you need to set boundaries right around your working hours? Same with the calendar: you set your own hours. Before you open your calendar to clients, you want to make sure that you have blocked out the days you want to take off. Or the recital date of your little one. Or the three-day getaways you have planned with your hubby. You put it all in there. And then what is left is open for the clients to book a time with you. That simple.

Last but not least, I like for my clients to have a form to prepare for their coaching call. I use Wufoo forms. I love this application as it is super easy. I believe there are other platforms out there, but I am happy with Wufoo. If a prospective client wants to have a pre-call with me (often referred to as a strategy session—this is the call where you figure out if the two of you are a good match and if you will moving forward with this prospect as a client), I get the candidate to fill out a pre-qualification form so that, on the call, we can get to the essentials.

Now the clients who are in coaching with me have to also fill out a form before every call. This allows us to stay focused and not lose time catching up, as the essentials are already in the form.

While you are doing all these steps, you want to also start growing your social media presence. Perhaps create a business page on Facebook, an Instagram account, or even both. You want to have a LinkedIn profile that is accurate and professional.

And you do not need to wait for your first client to have a social media presence. Start as soon as you can, perhaps just right after getting your business name and phone number. Because the truth is, you can coach anyone from anywhere!

This brings me to one more step: get a Zoom account. I always say that my backyard is the world, because I coach clients from all over the world. Thank you, Zoom! Zoom facilitates having clients everywhere in the world.

With Zoom, you have your own personal virtual room. Your client is sitting in the comfort of his home and you are sitting in your office, or in the comfort of your own home. You see each other. Or you don't (you can pick the option audio-only). Convenient, cheap, efficient, and there are not limitations to where your clients are located. Now don't get me wrong: you don't have to be able to see your client to coach them. Over the phone works quite well! I have been trained to hear what I am not seeing. When you see your client's face and reactions, you might interpret them one way or the other. When you are on the phone, you have to hear that reaction or that face the client is making. It is as if when you can't see your client, your sensory acuity is heightened.

I shared all these practical tools with you assuming that you have already a solid coaching certification in place. Or perhaps you are still working on your certification.

It is important to have the right certification. I did hours of research back in 2004 when I decided to become a coach. I went with the Life Purpose Institute. Later on, in 2014, I went with the Robbins and Madanes Training. (known as RMT). Once you are done with this latter training, you are certified as a Strategic Intervention Coach. And last but not least, I went through the top of the top coaching training academy to become a Results Coach for Robbins Research International. (I am not going to spend time on this last training with the coaching academy, as it is like an interview process and by invitation-only.)

There are certifications from $10 to over $10K. Seriously! And then there are all the people out there who present themselves as life coaches when their experience is just a few good conversations helping some friends. Sad. As you probably know, coaching is not a regulated industry just yet. Right now, anyone who can add an ICF certification to their coaching business will be golden. Honestly, no one has ever asked me what my certification was. At the end of the day, it is not a piece of paper and a title that count, it is the results you get for your clients that speak volumes.

Again, I have no affiliation whatsoever with the following suggestions:

Steve G. Jones offers a coaching certification for less than $100. The only reason I am even mentioning this one is because it is a great fit for anyone who is thinking of becoming a coach. It is an effective way to learn more about what coaching is and to learn basic tools. This short program is self-help and will get you clarity about if coaching is for you or not.

lifecoachingcertified.com

Life Purpose Institute (which has live and online program options) is a serious and intensive program you might want to look into. It is based on career and life purpose coaching. You will learn all the tools needed to coach someone.

https://www.lifepurposeinstitute.com

Another great one is with Christy Whitman, Quantum Coaching. Christy focuses more on the Universal laws and spiritual manifestation. Her school is a great place to start and get a solid foundation.

www.quantumcoachingessentials.com

Robbins Madanes Training is an online program. It is based on the interventions Tony Robbins does and, through watching these, you get to learn tools and strategies. It is well done, and you will have a more general foundation covering all areas of life such as health, relationships, finances, business-related coaching, etc.

https://rmtcenter.com/certification-programs/core-100/

When you are looking for a coaching certification you want to do your due diligence and make sure it is a solid program that will get you the results you are after. Don't settle for the lesser price. You want quality. Talk to people. Get some references.

Are you excited yet? There might be more tools to share around setting up the business, yet I promise you that by starting with this list, you will be way ahead. Have fun with it!

CHAPTER 13

WHEN IS *NOW* A GOOD TIME?

"It always seems impossible until it's done."
– Nelson Mandela

L et's be super honest and real for a minute here! It is not because you now have a plan, new tools, and strategies that you will be taking massive action.

You know, change is only possible when we are honest about where we are and what is really going on. I am not going to sugarcoat it for you: on this journey, there will be ups and downs. There will be obstacles! You will feel like you are moving two steps forward and taking three steps back.

About all these mindset tools I have shared along the way, I owe you the truth: it does not happen overnight! When you go to the gym and work with a trainer to set a goal and get the plan that will get you to the results you want to achieve, the truth is, it takes time and repetition. Right?

You go, day after day, even if you are tired, even if you do not see the results right away. And after a few weeks, you will start seeing results. You are developing your muscles. Now, if you take a few months' break, do you sincerely believe that when you go back at it you will be at the same level you were when you stopped? No.

These powerful mindset tools I shared with you along the way, you need to practice them every day. *When?* Every day! No matter what. It is vital.

Here is the thing though. Fear is going to kick in. And you are going to decide what definition you give it: False Evidence Appearing Real or F* Everything And Run.

Because you will feel like you want to run. You want to quit. The reality is that you are still here, reading this book. Give yourself a pat on the back. So many stopped before even starting.

Some quit as soon as it gets complicated. Some get discouraged because they do not see immediate results. Now, you. I believe you are different. I think you have what it takes to go after your dream. I believe you will do whatever it takes to make it happen. Well-intentioned people around you will tell you differently. Will question you. Will even put you down because of their own limitations and fears. But not you, dear reader. You are still here reading. I believe in you.

Every time you receive resistance from someone else or you feel resistance yourself, you need to check what limiting beliefs are coming up. Are you listening to facts or to fiction? Is your brain or someone else trying to protect you? This is a perfect opportunity to grow.

When you feel resistance, allow yourself to reconnect with your why, your purpose. The fuel increasing the fire in your belly to go after your dream. And once you reconnect with that, you will grow. You will feel stronger and stronger.

I have two different scenarios here for you.

Scenario A: When you have a limiting belief, you will not see the potential and infinite possibilities all around you. When you feel that there is limited potential, you will take minimum action and therefore have minimal or next to no results. And that will reinforce your limiting belief.

Scenario B: When you have a powerful belief, you will see the potential. From that place, you will take massive action, and this will create great results. Now your powerful belief is being reinforced even more.

Which scenario do you want to work from? Because Scenario B really seems like the perfect success cycle to adopt!

One more thing I need to mention here. You heard me earlier using the expression "Life happens *for* you" versus "life happens *to* you."

Well, here is a fact: when you step up, this is when the storm comes in! I have seen it countless times in my life and private practice. It is like you are being tested. It's the Universe's way to check if you are serious about achieving your goal. Testing you to see if you have what it takes to go for it.

The truth is you will be tested. Many times. In small ways and in big ways. Life will happen for you so you can learn in the process. The question is, how will you answer these tests?

You want to decide right now that no matter what, you are going to figure out a way to get that first client and open the new business.

Here is one of my absolute favorite tools for you. You want to become an expert at separating the problems from the symptoms. Another of my dear mentors, Keith Cunningham, shared this fantastic concept in one of the lectures I attended last year. This made all the difference for me.

If I were to ask you what your three most significant problems are right now in getting this business off the ground, you might share with me things like:

a. "I don't have a list," or
b. "I can't afford to pay for marketing," or even
c. "I need to get more certifications." Right?

The list can go on and on here. These things are not a problem. They are a description of the gap. The gap is not the problem; it really is the symptom.

And the symptom is there to show you that there is something wrong that needs to be taking care of. Yes, something is wrong with point a, b, and c, yet these things are not the root of the problem. You know what you want and what you don't have. And you think *that* is the root problem.

It is not. The key is to find the obstacle that is in the way of getting the results that you want. What happens? You ask questions that give you a tactical solution. And then you build a machine to solve the perceived problem (the symptom)—which means the machine is for a problem that is not.

Okay, I think I just lost you here! Let me give you some clarity: take for example how you might say to yourself, "People don't know me, I don't have a list, and I need to figure out how to put myself out there."

You will then build a machine. Here in my example, I am thinking of a website and probably upping your social media presence. Right? You will be utilizing resources and honestly wasting time and money that, I guarantee you, will not move you forward to your desired outcome.

I hear this so often among my clients. "My business is not where it needs to be. I don't have enough clients. I have decided to update my website and to create a new Facebook business page. And then it will be all okay!" Will it be okay? Really? No.

Because the lack of clients is a symptom of the problem. Changing the website is not going to make a difference. The question is, what is the obstacle, a.k.a. the real problem? When you can answer that for yourself, you will be unstoppable.

I cannot tell you how many pieces of fitness equipment I have bought in my life! I bought so many different ones and sold them a few months later. And I am still not at my desired weight. What happened? I misdiagnosed the problem by asking the wrong questions.

Doing so, I got tactical answers, and I bought equipment for a problem that really was not the real problem. I have a beautiful Street Strider in my garage. Oh, did I want it? I saved pennies after pennies to purchase that beautiful machine! Yet, I never addressed the core problem that is at the foundation of my ongoing yo-yo weight. I bet you can relate and might have done so yourself in various areas of your life.

I am begging you to really understand this concept, and when you find yourself going tactical, take a deep breath and start asking better questions to understand what the real problem is. This will save you quite a few headaches and precious resources such as time and money.

You might have noticed that, in all the tools shared, I did not mention building a website. Because the truth is, you don't need one to be successful. Is it helpful to have down the road? Or is it nice to have a professional page coming up when someone Googles your name?

Sure. It is not your website that will bring you clients. Neither will your mailing list. My mentor Dr. Angela Laura said in one of my trainings that, "Our list is really a parking lot for non-buyers." She calls it a "holding place for non-buyers." It has very little to no value.

Your clients are going to be people who you are just going to meet, not someone who has been on your email list for months. Very rare. (Of course, the exception confirms the rule.)

Your clients are going to be people coming through word of mouth, referrals mostly, and people who want to work with you, because of…*you*. That something about you that makes them feel that by working with you, they are in good hands. They know in their guts that you can guide them in achieving their dreams. You have had the results for yourself and for others, and they trust you!

Stop worrying about not having a list, or not having a website or even a social media presence. It is not worth your time and energy!

CHAPTER 14

CONCLUSION

*"Know what sparks the light in you. Then
use that light to illuminate the world."*
– Oprah Winfrey

Do you have people in your life that you trust? Like, when
you ask them to do something you know without a shadow
of a doubt that they will do that one thing? You trust them, and
you can relax and know that the thing you asked about is going
to be taken care of no matter what? Great. And I will get back
to that thought in a moment.

Now, what would happen if you set out for yourself very
high expectations to be successful? To expect a successful launch
and these first clients signing up with you? You have learned
a lot of tools and strategies in this book. You have done the
work. But it does not stop here. I am excited you are still here,

reading these last few pages, and my wish for you is that now you understand the power of the 80/20 formula.

Success is eighty percent mindset and twenty percent strategies. You have received numerous mindset tools to use on your journey to create the life you want and open that new business.

Earlier in the book, I covered the power of manifesting what your heart desires and the importance of having clarity and being aligned to the outcome you want to achieve. Being in a state of allowing and a state of non-resistance.

Here it is time to add one final piece to that: when you have high expectations, it is like you have your foot on the accelerator pedal. You want to find the right balance between your desires and expectations and being detached. Don't be too specific with these expectations, just wake up every morning knowing that you are doing your part, that the Universe is working on your behalf, and that you will be successful no matter what. If you step into fear and focus on the lack of progress or try to control every step of the way, it would be the equivalent of you stepping on the brake pedal.

Now, one foot on the accelerator and one on the brake is not going to get you moving far! The key is not to "let go" and hope that it is all going to work out. The key is to "give it" to someone you trust. To a higher power. To the Universe. To your God.

Like I shared at the beginning of this chapter, when you trust someone, you can relax, right? Here is the same attitude to have: you set your precise expectations, you believe that what you're asking for will happen—or even better—and you detach yourself by doing your part and knowing in your heart all is going to be alright.

It is a delicate balance that takes time to master. But I believe in you, and I know that by applying a minimum of twenty percent of the tools shared in this book, you will be creating eighty percent of the results you are after.

This does not mean "apply the tools once." No, it means every single day. It is about managing your state and your emotions every day.

Remember the concept of creating breakthroughs? It always starts with asking yourself, "Who do I need to be?" and from there creating a powerful state. Then you can create a new story and focus on strategies to put in place.

Step into the truth of who you are. Reach for all the tools and answers that are already within you. I wish for you to believe in yourself and to become more resourceful. Resources are never the problem—what is needed is resourcefulness! And resourcefulness starts with the right mindset. I wish for you to understand that the tools you have learned in this book will absolutely transform your life.

You are now equipped to handle any situations coming your way. You have a menu of options to pick from that will guarantee success and growth.

Remember that you are not alone. When you are ready to take it to the next level and to put your success on turbo, reach out via my website and let's continue this conversation. Let me help you like I have helped many other clients like you open their own coaching businesses.

This is really the final piece: start by doing what you are about to ask people to do—hire a coach. You've got this. You came this far and read the book all the way to the end. That says a lot about you. I believe in you.

ACKNOWLEDGMENTS

I have always had a drive for learning, personal growth, and lifting others along the way. I was the kid hiding under the blanket with a flashlight reading late into the night. I was a friend with a shoulder to cry upon for support. I have always been passionate about finding ways to continually grow. This book has been long in the making. I have dreamed of this book for years. I gave it so many titles, wrote so many chapters in my head. Until, inspired by my sister Veronique, I said, "Enough is enough, now it is time to do what you said you were going to do."

I am grateful for my amazing family and for all the support from my husband. Thank you for believing in me honey! I want to recognize my four amazing children, Michael, Jimmy, Sixtine, and Olivia. Thank you for believing in me and loving me through the constant work, the stress, and the long hours. I am so proud of each of you, and I could not have dreamed of better kids than you. I smile at the memory of you telling me, "Mom, I really need to talk to my mom right now, not the coach." And here we are: I watch you growing and using many of the tools shared with you along the way. My life is blessed just because of every single one of you.

To my colleagues and mentors. The power of our team is incredible, and it keeps me going every day. This is one safe place where I know I can go for support or to even discuss a "worthy opponent." Not only do I gain tremendous experience and knowledge while working with you, but I have also gained fantastic friendships. Thank you, team, for being there and allowing me to show up vulnerable.

Thank you to my work wife, Mandi. You and I have shared so many insights and gone through a lot together. You taught me the power of smiling and connecting with others even after a nineteen-hour day! You always pushed me to better myself and to step up the game no matter what. You have impacted my life through your coaching, your love, and your authenticity. You have truly inspired me to become more every day. Thank you not judging me when I fell asleep while ten thousand people were dancing around me. That was epic!

Cheryll: thank you for your loving and spiritual guidance. My life is more abundant just because of you. I cannot see myself not having you in my life. Thank you for always being there and answering present!

And finally, my amazing clients, too many to name each one of you. It is an honor to serve you and to watch you grow and experience breakthroughs. I love being on this journey with you, and I thank you for playing full out. What you might not realize is that coaching you forces me to continually step up and stretch myself. It fills my heart to be there for you.

Thank you to Angela Lauria and The Author Incubator's team, as well as to David Hancock and the Morgan James Publishing team for helping me bring this book to print.

THANKS FOR READING

Thank you for reading this book and playing full out! I appreciate each and every one of you who opened this book and committed to reading it from the introduction to the conclusion.

As a thank you, I've created a bonus for you. Send me an email with a subject line "Ready for Your Bonus" and I will email you a PDF file with guidelines on getting clarity around setting up a scalable business model.

As you know by now, one of my favorite sayings is, "When is now a good time to start?" Right? It is essential to never leave the site of a decision without taking action.

So here is my contact info to continue this journey.

Don't hesitate to reach out through my website, www.resultsnow.coach, or send me an email at carine@resultsnow.coach.

Facebook: https://www.facebook.com/resultsnowcoach/
Website: https://www.resultsnow.coach
LinkedIn: https://www.linkedin.com/in/carinekindinger/
Twitter: https://twitter.com/ResultsNowCoach

ABOUT THE AUTHOR

 Carine Kindinger is a Results Coach and Business Results Trainer for Robbins Research International. She also owns Results Now Coaching (www.resultsnow. coach). She has been coaching clients since 2004, when she took the risk to quit her corporate job and follow her passion for helping others succeed through coaching. Carine's personal mission is to empower people to live to their highest potential by giving them the tools they need to do so. She helps her clients develop individual plans to achieve anything they want in their lives, working on everything from their careers to their health to their relationships. At the end of the day, it is all about getting clarity, having the right mindset to achieve anything we set our minds to.

Carine moved to the United States from Belgium in 2000, starting her life over (and bringing her delightful accent with her) in search of a better life in the States. Since then, she has built multiple businesses up from foundation to profitability and has pushed through countless challenges. Her own life has been an example of the impossible becoming possible, and she is passionate about her clients experiencing the same thing. She understands what it takes to thrive in any economy and through the challenges of any type of business.

Carine became certified as a life purpose coach through the Life Purpose Institute in 2004. She revolutionized her practice when she added the Robbins Madanes Training to her toolbelt and became a Strategic Intervention Coach. Carine then went on through an intensive World Class Coaching Academy qualification process to become a Results Coach, coaching people to create breakthroughs and results in every area of their lives. She coaches her clients using personal insights as well as the knowledge gained from the constant intensive training she participates in.

Carine's journey has motivated her to inspire her clients to live the life they desire—both personally and professionally. She believes that with the power of manifestation and the right state of mind, her clients can be successful in achieving their goals. Carine herself is her own success story.

Carine currently resides in Texas with her husband and four dogs, but she often says that the world is her backyard as her clients are located all over the world. She is blessed with four kids, three step-kids, and six grandchildren. She loves nature, and one of her favorite things to do before starting her day is to just sit in silence, watching birds, dogs, and nature wake up. She loves sun and water and takes every opportunity to travel to places where she can enjoy both.

CPSIA information can be obtained
at www.ICGtesting.com
Printed in the USA
JSHW011440271020
9157JS00002B/99

9 781642 799668